# TALES FROM

# THE Sand

# HILLS

# Tales from the Sand Hills

A Collection of Short Stories

FROM THE PEN OF MARY SEATON
OF TIBOOBURRA

BALBOA.
PRESS

A DIVISION OF HAY HOUSE

Balboa Press books may be ordered through booksellers or by contacting:

Balboa Press
A Division of Hay House
1663 Liberty Drive
Bloomington, IN 47403
www.balboapress.com.au
1-(877) 407-4847

ISBN: 978-1-4525-0390-5 (sc)
ISBN: 978-1-4525-0391-2 (e)

Printed in the United States of America

Balboa Press rev. date: 01/25/2012

Around the campfire burning low, yet still gives off a warming glow
Down on the ever warming ground, the weary men sat all around
They passed some time at idle play, that holds the loneliness at bay
And they tell tales of days gone by, while stars looked on in blackened sky
As Bushmen dream in swags remote the dingoes howl their eerie note
And God alone stands watch at night, beside that camp fire burning bright
There aint no angels to lend a hand, out there in no man's land

To Roland Batt for whom this book was written

# Contents

# About the author

Rosanna Mary Hoppo 2010

Born Rosanna Mary Seaton in Pemberton WA.

The daughter of a rabbit trapper (returned war hero) she grew up travelling all over Australia. She was educated to high school standard doing correspondence (school of the air). Along with her sister Judith Seaton was taught by their mother Maida. At age fourteen she was sent to boarding school in Broken Hill and left school at end of year twelve. Growing up in the great Australian outback her parents' based themselves out of Tibooburra and this she adopted as her home town. She married in South Australia and all her children were born in that state. Rosanna went on to become a truck driver until she could no longer do it and then became a security guard and worked up on the Olympic Dam mine. She started writing in her late forties.

# A Life Begun

My name is Rosanna Mary Seaton; I live now in Pt. Pirie in South Australia. I was born Rosanna Mary Seaton in Pemberton Western Australia in 1954. With my parents Arthur and Maida and my sister Judith. I lived all over Australia, mostly in the great Australian outback. At age seven my brother Bruce was born in the Broken Hill hospital in New South Wales.

I have always considered myself very fortunate and privileged to have had the opportunity to grow up among such wonderful people and in such a place. And what an honor it was to have known the friends I met along the way both human and animal. I also consider it a pleasure to introduce these friends, alive and deceased to you all as I will do in the in the next few pages.

My father (deceased) was Robert Arthur Seaton of Sandy Creek in Victoria. He was a returned war vet. And could not settle back into life on the family farm. Comes to that he could not settle anywhere. He had spent six years in the Second World War which he served with the second eighth battalion in Europe and the middle east down through

Timor and finally in New Guinea. A commando, he was a distinguished soldier who had won medals of valor while fighting for his country.

He met my mother, a quiet but very strong farm girl and together they headed off to start a new life in Western Australia where my sister and I Were born. From there they launched a life and times which compares equally to most.

My sister and I were schooled by correspondence or 'the school of the air' as it is better known. I started school in Queensland but the first real school I went to was down in Victoria while dad was doing some work down there back in 1960. We went to school for almost a year before we returned to our beloved sand hills and Queensland.

Travelling North was written about this journey. I don't know what it is about the sand hills that tugs on my heart strings but tug they did. It is a hard country up there and very unforgiving to anyone who underestimates it. I touched on this in my story 'A Walk in the Desert'.

During a drought these hills become bare and are a magnificent red color. They will be dotted with trees of a very hardy nature but they shift during these times, their sands being whipped up and carried by the winds. My dad once buried a bottle full of one five and ten pound notes while he left for a trip. When he returned he couldn't find it because the sand had shifted. So that is probably still there for all you treasure hunters.

During the droughts the country is burned by the sun and the hot north winds relentlessly. The cattle die and other livestock. Wild life dies or disappears. The land becomes burnt and baron, the water dries up and there are only bores to rely on.

Cattle get bogged in the muddy waters of the drying up dams and will die if they're not pulled free. As feed becomes scarce and water disappears the cattle can do nothing but lie down and perish in the searing sun. Sometimes the only thing you can do is to go out and shoot the poor devils so as not to prolong their great suffering. The only kindness you could do for the poor cows is to shoot them first so they never see what you have to do to their babies.

That said, mostly they make it through the dry until the rains come. And when the rains do come the country undergoes a complete transformation. Almost overnight the vegetation grows back, enough grass for everyone. The red sand is covered once more in green grasses and wildflowers of red ll of these birds will and yellow and white, even mauve. The old spinifex bushes which have held on all through the drought are rewarded for their tenacity.

Clay pans, creeks and dams are filled with water. Lakes fill up and water roars through creeks and catchment areas. Frogs spring to life and sing their song of joy to all who were there to listen. Soon the waters would be teaming with tadpoles.

The smell of the rain the wet earth and the leaves of all the plants as they opened themselves to the water, the beautiful life giving water.

The wild life returns to the desert transformed into paradise, as if they'd been waiting just round the bend. Animals appear and start frolicking and running as if stretching their stiff cramped limbs.

As the rain slows to a mist a cool refreshing mist after months sometimes even years of heat and harsh dryness, animals come out of hiding to drink and vent their joy. At such times as these I have seen the brolgas dance their beautiful graceful dance and no better praise to heaven have I ever seen.

Soon the lakes and creeks are teeming with bird, emus, pelicans, swans, cockies, gahlas, plovers and dozens of other varieties. The old crow is there and the magpies and the noise is wonderful. The brolgas to of course and wild turkeys, all move to the water's edge.

Soon enough all of these birds will get down to the business of producing offspring. The rabbits pour back into the country and that is where my dad comes in because he is a rabbiter. He catches rabbits and sells them for a living.

We lived in a caravan for most of my child hood as we travelled around the country following them. We sold rabbits overseas and all over Australia. The last time I sold a pair of rabbits was in 1968 and I got 40cents a pair.

My mother loved the life in the outback even though it went from hard to extremely hard. She cooked on an open fire mostly and we washed by hand. I was ten years old before we lived in a house in town and enjoyed electricity for the first time.

As young as I was I was always glad to get back up to the bush. During the war my mum worked in 'munitions. She was also my first teacher and may I say a very strict one. Anytime we were sent to school it was always commented on how well we were taught and how far ahead we were.

I always get back up the bush whenever I can and things are changing out there. There are much better roads now thanks to the large mining and oil drilling outfits. When I was a kid there were only tracks and a day's trip today would take weeks back then.

With the roads came progress and now there are shops, roadhouses hotels caravan parks etc. where once there was only scrub. Tourists have taken the place of most of the animals. My parents passed away many years ago and I often wonder what they would make of it all now.

Anyhow I guess it will become clear to you all as you read these pages that I love the great Australian outback and I have the utmost respect for it. Even today you can regret not respecting her. She made me laugh, she made me cry and she taught me right from wrong. She gave me love and she gave me danger and at times she broke my heart. And may I say that I would not change a single day of my childhood.

And the friends I met along the way shall remain forever in my heart. Thanks for the memories and thanks for the times you took pity on me and spared my life. I am absolutely certain that I shall return to her for my long sleep.

Anyhow, without farther ado, welcome to my life and I hope you get something from my story.

# Chapter 1

## TALES FROM THE SAND HILLS

The fog was thick that morning, what the English people might call a real pea souper and as cold a morning as I can ever remember. Up there in the red sand hills of the desert country the cold winds of the morning just seemed to go straight though to your bones. The sun was just up and everything smelt fresh even though we couldn't see too much. From one Spinifex bush to another was about what we were doing as we made our way through them.

My sister walked beside me as we went on our way to the next trap. We'd only got one rabbit so far and only had two traps to go so things were a bit dismal all round. One rabbit out of twenty traps!

My feet ached with the cold and all the three corner jacks and cannon ball thistles I'd walked on. Cannon balls are a small round ball, found only in outback Queensland I think, with hard sharp spikes on them and boy did they hurt when you stepped in 'em. They just seemed to slide right on through your flesh as if they were needles dipped in oil.

In actual fact, needles wouldn't hurt as much. They were worse than the three corner jacks because of their size and they had more spikes.

'What I wouldn't give for a pair of blinkin' shoes' I said as much to myself as to Judith. Our shoes had worn out months ago and it would be still some months before we went to town again. This was only July.

We went to Broken Hill every Christmas for a week or so and we loved it. We always had fish and chips for tea that was the only time we ever got fish or chips. We also got coke to drink and potato chips and some chocolate. We got none of these things the rest of the year and we always went home sick in the stomach. In fact mum always got Dad to buy a bottle of the dreaded soda water as we were leaving.

'Yeah my oath' she said 'and a nice one of those jackets like we saw in that magazine remember? I'll have the blue one an' you can have the pink one.'

'Nuh. I'm havin' the blue one,' I said, not because I particularly liked blue but to stir her up a bit. Things were a bit quiet like an' I was feeling peculiarly nervous this morning for some reason I couldn't fathom. As she opened her mouth to argue I put in 'else I'll tell mum you kissed Russel.'

I felt a little bad about the look of sorrow on her face so I decided to shut up for once. At eleven years of age, I guessed that Russel may have been her one true love and we'd had to leave him far behind in Victoria as my father and mother left to chase rabbits round the country side. We'd lived in almost every state by the time we were school age. Anyway we left Russel behind and headed for Queensland to the corner country. The rabbits are lousy up there we were told and dad couldn't pack up quick enough. We loved Queensland for some reason or other. Tibooburra had become my home town so to speak but that's over the border in NSW.

Anyway, to alleviate the boredom and bad feeling I'd created with my big mouth and the cold that actually hurt I put my head back and howled the howl of a dingo. A bloody dingo itself couldn't tell that was a human I thought as I listened to my sister do the same. Nope, not even a dingo would suspect that wasn't a dingo either. Smiling pleased with myself, all was well again.

It felt real good so we kept it up for a bit then fell silent again as we trudged on far from home. I went on in front a little bit and left my sister to her private thoughts.

Don't suppose I'll ever have one of those jackets I thought, not as long as I live. Jee whizz its cold, wish I had a pair of pants to that'd keep my legs warm. What's the chance of that ever happening I asked myself dismally?

Suddenly, another howl that brought me to a stand still and raised the hair on the back of my neck, I spun round and looked at Judith with awe.

'That was the best ever' I said and the grin slid from my dile at the look on her face. Her eyes were trying to tell me something.

'That was you Judith?' I cried at her as I felt the style of my breathing change slightly. 'Wasn't it?' I whispered, steam hanging on the air as I spoke.

'I know it was you' she replied trying to grin, but we'd come to a standstill leaning forwards, eyes straining to see through the heavy fog. I shook my head. 'Dingoes' we both breathed at the same time.

'Run' my sister shouted but my legs had frozen stiff and not from the cold either. She shot passed me, 'come on Mary for heavens sake!'

I tried to but no, my damn legs still didn't want to obey me.

'Come on legs or I'll leave you behind' I shouted as I set off at a very slow and very awkward run. You try running when you're terrified. Not only do your legs go stiff but they seem to stick out at odd angles from your hips. I was losing all feeling from my knees to the ground.

Then I heard it again, closer, probably not a hundred yards in front. Not only was the damn thing stalking us but it was between us and home.

I made a mental note that I would never make their sounds again, nor would I ever harass them again in any way if god would just help me out of this spot.

We changed direction slightly to try and go round where we'd heard him. Another howl directly in front changed our direction again and left us with an awful feeling of dread that there now appeared to be at least two of the buggers. However the next howl from just over my right shoulder from a third party leant wings to my feet and I shot passed my sister like she was standing still.

The traps were forgotten and our one and only rabbit was lying back there somewhere on the ground, dingoes fodder! Hardly even worth remembering at a time like this.

By now we were running at almost right angles to home and following the sand hill along. Spinifex bushes hampered our going and scratched us relentlessly if we couldn't quite make the jump. I got my sleeve caught on a mulga tree branch and left a piece of that behind not even making a mental note that I was in trouble for that. Mum'd informed me that morning that this jumper was the only one I had left without a hole in it.

We had to get across the valley somehow and to the safety of the caravan and mum. We knew we could follow the sand hill for a ways but pretty soon by my calculations we'd be level with the caravan and home. We'd have to make a break for it and maybe cut across the path of the dingo or dingos.

I could hear my sister's labouring breath behind me and hoped she'd keep up the pace. She'd always had trouble with her breathing. I stole a look over my shoulder, she was probably gaining on me if anything but I could see her clearly in the fog and I knew what was on her mind.

This is it I thought, time to go and I changed direction, straight across the valley, praying to a God I never usually bothered with and didn't know much about but I knew he liked kids. I sure hoped he did! I'll be good I promised, from now on.

One more, loud howl behind us, just behind us, and my sister caught up. 'Holy cow' I muttered as she drew alongside me, 'we be in trouble all right!'

My lungs were starting to protest to and I started thinking to myself, I don't remember this valley being this wide. I stole another look over my shoulder and what I saw was awesome. Four magnificent dingos, loping along lazily, my feet slowed. The fog had cleared considerably now and I saw the dingos slow and turn round and head off back the way we'd come.

I turned back to the front, mouth as wide open as my eyes now and saw why they'd made that decision. Home! Right in front of us. Made it!

We could see home as clear as a bell now just up in front of us. I hit the skids about the same instant as my sister. We stopped to get our breath.

'Not a word.' We both said at once. 'Let's not tell Mum or dad or anyone OK?' My sister went on.

I nodded, ok by me. Damn right! Imagine being afraid of a pack of mangy old dingos. We'd be a laughing stock for sure wouldn't we I wondered? Best keep quiet and not find out.

Well anyway there was Mum smiling at us from the fire. 'Get anything?' she asked.

Hadn't thought of that now had we? Hadn't occurred to us that someone might ask us that. We looked at each other then back to mum.

'No!' we spoke in unison. I knew my face was red and I felt just awful

'Ooh that's no good.' She said sympathetically, only adding to my discomfit.

'No. What's for brekkie?' I asked trying to appear nonchalant. All thoughts of dingos pushed to the back of my mind. All thoughts of dingos, God, my promise, everything. All Gone.

But I was hungry, my stomach was growling for food. Amazing what an early morning workout and a bit of terror will do for your appetite. 'What's for brekkie?' I asked my mum who was bent over the fire, 'and where is it?'

'I haven't got it ready yet' she replied patiently.

'Why not?' I demanded, still puffed up from my brush with the dingo. My win over the dingos!

'Because I haven't' she said trying to remain patient but her voice showing some strain if I'd only had the sense to listen. But I wasn't finished with her so I plunged on.' Well what've you been doing all this time?' I asked. 'Sittin' around?'

As she looked up at me I suspected I may have gone a bit far with that last crack. She stood up and pulled a sapling twig from a nearby tree. I could feel another fast jog coming on.

'By the livin' Harry you just wait till I get hold of you, you cheeky little vixen.' She turned back to me her face livid.

Chrikey! Once again that morning I was running for my life only this time I didn't hold out much hope. But I set off anyway, running as fast as I could from my mother who was hot on my heels. And I knew what she could do with a sapling stick and I knew I'd made her fairly mad.

I looked over my shoulder and realised with great surprise that she was gaining on me. She was about an arms length behind.

I cast a glance over to my right and decided to try outrunning her up the sand hill there. It was steep and it was high, 'she won't catch me going up that' I says to myself and changed direction. My mother offered what encouragement she could with some details of what she was gonna do to me when she got her hands on me.

I reached the bottom of the sand hill and started to climb, I was always so quick on my feet climbing sand hills and I knew it was my best chance

Of outrunning her.

She changed direction to and came after me mumbling all the while about what she was going to do to me if she caught me. I knew I was in trouble to make a normally soft hearted woman carry on like that!

Then the impossible happened, she fell. Just as she started to climb the damned sand hill she fell forward and as she put her hand out to save herself she caught me by the ankle. Pure luck!

I was dragged unceremoniously back down the hill and towards the sapling stick. My mother belted me round the legs with it all the way home to the laughing and loud applause of all the men standing round at the chiller watching my humiliation turn to pain. Quickly!

When I got home I wasn't quite so hungry. Maybe just a little bit of food just to show her how much she'd upset me and how my legs hurt I'd eat it real slow like.

I packed my things sadly, slowly into a sugar bag (after breakfast), tied a knot in the top and with all the drama I could muster I told my family I would be leaving and they would probably never see me again.

They all said goodbye and laughed unrestrainedly once again at my humiliation. I was back before sundown and all was forgotten, my parents never carried these things on. And the old dingos were just playing with us, probably laughed all the way home to. Well at least everyone got a laugh didn't they? Well cheers and thanks for caring. See you in the next tale.

# Chapter 2

## BRANDING TIME

Branding! Only one of the worst jobs you can do. It's hot, it's dangerous and it's very hard work. Physically there's not much harder work around. Usually its hot work to and dusty, very dusty and smoky to.

Anyway we're off to brand some cattle. Cattle I might add who are as wild as the desert country hills they inhabit. Some of them have never even seen man before, or women or kids, let alone learnt to get along. Back to the job. First you have to go after some beast right, some huge hairy psycho beast that everything from your brains to your bowels is telling you, you don't want to catch. To run in the opposite direction would be good.

And then having got the poor beast onto the ground, and that's a struggle all on its own, then you have to secure him there lest he get back up and kill you because he sure don't want to thank you. And these guys are huge usually with long sharp horns and I am no matador. I have no aspiration towards bullfighting what so ever.

Then he gets a brand burnt onto his butt the smell of which is quite sickening. And some of these animals take exception to that; I mean it's very painful I'm thinking. And again, some of these beasts take it personally; that their rear end has been badly burned like this and so when they start lookin' for revenge they don't just single out the guy with the branding iron, they see all of us.

Anyway I reckon you get the picture. Here we are in the heat and the flies, oh the flies! Especially round water or if there's rain coming and they get sticky. You practically have to drag 'em away from your face. And if you've ever slept near water out in these places you'll know why I mention the mossies.

I never took to a hat with a veil and so I've eaten my share of flies let me tell you. In fact I got to thinking that tryin' to get em back up was just not worth the struggle. Call me gross. I always did try to avoid swallowing them but that just makes you more crook tryin to heave em out like that. And my money's always been on the fly. By my calculations, you get em back up about twenty percent of the time so I guess it's up to the individual as to whether it's worth going for it or not.

Then all night long in your swag, that's nearly always too hot to sleep in, the mossies come a callin' and they don't wanna go home hungry either. Some nights when I've had the luxury of a mosquito net to sleep in, the noise has kept me awake. There's not much worse than trying to sleep while you're wondering where they're going to strike next.

Anyway the little mongrels just bight and bight all night. And you try to hit em and you whack yourself in the face hard only to listen to em breeze off again while your eye or your nose or whatever is still smarting from where you just hit it. So the battle in the blanket continues on from where the battle with the flies left off. I seldom bounced out of my swag rearin' to go.

I often wonder if aliens were watching us smacking ourselves like that right and they had no experience of insects at all. What the hell would they think?

And the water was the worst thing. Every time we moved camp out there in the bush we'd have to drink from a different bore. Now for those with no imagination I'll spell it out this way. D-i-a-r-r-h-o-e-a.

Sometimes the tank we'd have to drink from the water would be green with dead birds in it. The only way you could drink it was to boil it first. No bottled water out there then and no soft drinks either. We drank a lot of tea mate, a whole lot of tea. We drank it hot, cold, lukewarm, with sugar, without sugar, milk, no milk and now and again we'd switch to coffee.

A trip to the bore was usually an exciting event however, trying to get some water while these wild cattle came to observe. They didn't take too kindly to people near their water supply. Usually a few Hail Mary's and a couple of the Lord's prayers would just about do it. Well I'm still here, though whether that's by accident or design I've got no way of knowing til I get there.

Back to the job. One time, I was ten years old but I remember it well, we had this big bull on the ground he'd just been branded and I think from memory in full view of the rest of the herd.

Well he just lay there like he was dying or something and I remember thinking what a sissy he was when even the little guys got straight back up again. The men set him free from his hobble but he still lay there on the ground, breathing pretty normal.

Old Tom and Jacky and Geoff decided to roll themselves a smoke sittin' round the old land rover while we waited to see how the old bull was gonna fair. He lay still. Breathing in and out, in and out.

His front leg began to twitch and so did my rear end. Jeez! I reached back to feel the security of the old land rover. Next instant I was in it.

He was up, how the hell he got up that quick I don't know. I don't care to know. It was bedlam! The old bull let out a bellow and pawed the dirt once and came on down.

I was in the back of that land rover before the men hell I was up in the back of that thing before me! Jacky and Geoff jumped up in the back and old Tom jumped in the front. Old Tom went straight for the starter button to get us movin' and out of there.

Now on those old long wheel base land rovers, you might remember you had to turn the ignition key on that was down to the left and then hit the starter button which was down to your right. They were a mighty old bus to the old land rover I might add.

Anyhow on this particular occasion she wouldn't start. We up in the back didn't realise it but old Tom had forgotten the key. Over and over she whirred. Old Tom was apparently thinking how she'd just been serviced and should be starting first bloody pop. Then he said a couple of prayers, he told us later could only remember grace and we all know how that goes. 'For what we are about to receive . . . etc.'

Meanwhile the old bull's, just workin' himself up into a sweat. He got his left horn under the wheel arch of the old rover and was heaving us up into the air trying to tip it over. And very nearly succeedin' to I might add. Whirr whirr. Expletin deletents. The bull snorting and bellowing the sound of the rover as she drops back onto the dirt. Sheer bloody terror!

Geoff, good old Uncle Geoff sprang up with a shovel in his hand and hit that bull on the head. Bull didn't even notice. Jeez I was glad about that. I couldn't see how annoying him was gonna make the situation any better. Shovel looked like a teaspoon.

I tried to poke myself into the toolbox under the back window and when that didn't work I tried shuttin' my eyes. That was worse. The sound was just awful and the smell! And the bulls' rear still stunk to. Funny the things you think about when your about to meet your maker, it was like just sittin' there marking time.

Uncle Geoff landed back in the tray I don't know how many times but he always got back up. Now was he a brave man or just a fool? I will leave that to you. But there he was belting this huge bull over the head with a shovel. I think the bull was more intent on killing the rover than he was on trying to shake us out of it. Maybe not.

The whirr, whirr turned into the heavenly sound of a motor, music to my ears, old Tom had remembered to turn the bloody key. The bull let the rover fall and drew away for a second look. The motor had surprised him to. Well anyway we took the opportunity to get the hell away from there for a while, until he cooled off a bit.

Now whenever I hear that saying they charge like wounded bulls' I can't help but think 'or a bull with a sore backside.' The thing I took away from that day was that I probably wouldn't make a good cowgirl. I probably wouldn't make any sort of cowgirl.

Although later in life I got a farm and started breeding Herefords and I loved my beautiful red girls with their cute white faces. But then I had them from babies so we were well used to each other, I'd bottle fed them for weeks.

For a little while I had a little red bull who was a playful little bloke. I also had a grumpy little Chihuahua and the bull was always trying to get a game going with the dog but he wouldn't be in it.

Anyway cheers people and thanks for letting me get this off my chest it's been great therapy. And remember;

'For what we are about to receive may the Lord make us truly thankful.' Amen 'n' By now.

# Chapter 3

# CHRISTMAS ROLLS ROUND AGAIN

Whenever I think of Christmas I think of Christmas trees decorated with shiny, colorful balls and tinsel. The tinkle of the piano and beautiful voices singing carols. Of summer holidays, mouth watering aromas and a certain magic that a man in a red suit could inspire in us all. Reindeers and snow although I have never actually seen snow.

Well this one Christmas stands out by a mile and though I was only seven at the time I remember it like it was yesterday. We always made the trip down to Broken Hill for our Christmas; we had done since I was five I think. That was the first time I'd seen a big town and or eaten fish and chips or tasted coke or any other sought of soft drink. I had my first ice cream to when I was five. It's nice to be able to remember these things.

Dad took us to a café, it was called the Ozone Café, and we had fish and chips. I do recall a lot of gutsing went on on these trips and was always followed by awful sick stomachs. My sister was worse than me

16

she always got sick. Funny that because I was usually the sickly one of the family.

The next night we were treated to the pictures and I was awe struck. I remember mum took me to my first picture show. It was a western, she loved them, and there was a lot of shooting and men falling off their horses. Mum asked me why I was crying and I told her that it was so sad that these men gave their lives for a movie. That got a few laughs back at the pub. We always stayed at the Wilcannia Club Hotel the Trengroves who had it had become friends. All the bushies stayed there. The who's who of the back blocks.

So coming down to the Hill at Christmas time had become sort of a tradition. The Christmas of '63, we had come down for Christmas but dad lost a lot of money at the two up so we had to leave a bit early. We returned to Tibooburra and spent Christmas there. It was great because we got to go to a fancy dress party in the hall and I had never seen one before.

I remember I saw this boy there dressed as Charlie Chaplain and I fell head over heels in love only to discover later that it was a bloody girl! Enough of that huh, no more of that I says to myself and stuck to it for years. But you know, even the best laid plans . . . Now after the fancy dress there was a dance on, you know the ones, all the girls sit round the hall and wait for those guys who are still sober enough to ask em for a dance. To hell with that to I say but they seemed keen.

It was around midnight I think and the pub and the dance hall next door were in full swing. My dad was drinking in the bar with some mates and mum was drinking outside with some women listening to the music.

No one actually noticed Curly leave with Mr. and Mrs. Pittmar and head off up into the rocks at the north end of town where they were camped. People used to camp up there in the rocks for some reason, we did to. Don't know why it was so popular.

Mr. Pittmar was a very jealous type and got very agro when he was inebriated. Mr. Pittmar was also a 'roo shooter and thus a very good shot and he never went anywhere without his rifle. I suppose we have to be fair and say that Mrs. Pittmar also liked to get inebriated and she liked to get amorous. Mr. Pittmar was a jealous type and well . . . The two didn't mix real well if you see what I mean.

Now a fight had broken out a bit earlier over a woman in pink tights and someone called the policeman. The two men defending her honour made up and went their merry way. I guess they were thirsty and headed back into the bar.

Meanwhile one of dad's mates gets into an argument and invites the offender outside. Off they go and straight into the arms of the policeman who was coming for the woman in the pink tights and the two offenders. Well he got these two into the paddy wagon instead. It's all very complicated I know.

The police man was tied up trying to sort this problem out back at the station see when the shots rang out. First one shot then another, a pause for a minute and then two more shots. They were coming from the direction of the rocks and were no doubt from a three 0 three.

People tumbled out into the street from the two pubs and the dance hall, parents searched around for their kids and kids searched round for their parents. Chaos.

A hush settled over the crowd then and another shot rang out. People craned their necks to look in that direction. From the darkness came the sound of boots running down the road towards us, and they were running fast. Then there came the sound of very heavy breathing. 'Jesus' cried one of the blokes, 'who the hells shootin' at who?'

Dad's mate Curly ran into the light his face as white as a sheet' his pants in one hand his shirt in the other and, save for his boots; he was as naked as the day he was born. Anyhow, he ran right on by and disappeared into the dark much to the delight of the crowd.

'Nice boots Curls' my dad sang out. The crowd howled their delight at poor old Curly and as many wisecracks as they had time to.

Any way all the hootin' and hollerin' stopped suddenly as another of dads mates ran into the bar with an object in his hand which looked suspiciously like a gun. As he passes through the door he shouts 'I've always wanted to do this' and proceeded to shoot up the bar.

The policeman was apparently out looking for the woman in the pink tights when he ran into Curly and ran Curly in. Back at the pub, Tommy Emptied his gun harmlessly into the mirror behind the bar and everyone got back to drinking.

When the copper got there a half hour or so later there was no sign of any gun and they told him that my dad had broken the mirror 'because the ugly old bastard looked in it.' Well he made some witty rejoinder which was drowned out in more insults from the crew. The publican scowled and shrugged his shoulders and somebody bought the policeman a drink.

Curly never told what he was doing on the bed with Mrs. Pittmar without a stitch on but he claims it was all very innocent. And who knows where Tommys' gun got to!

I heard years later he'd done the same thing in another little pub just outside Broken Hill. He didn't get caught then either. OK but no one was hurt and that is the main thing. Except for Curly, whose pride was gravely injured and he'd lost his socks and underwear back at the rocks.

I guess now when I think of Christmas I have to include guns, naked men and women in pink tights.

Anyway, don't let it bother you, I guess if Santa can wear a big heavy red suit with big boots in that heat and get about the sky on a team of reindeers and come down your chimney, well . . . Well, merry Xmas to all when it comes round again hay, in the meantime . . . keep your shirt on!

# Chapter 4

# A MOTHERS LOT

My mother's name was Maida Pfeiffer she was born in Victoria where she lived until she met my dad. You probably gathered from her name that she was of German descent. She passed away just under thirty years ago and I miss her still.

Though she was of German descent she loved the royal family and couldn't get enough of them. She loved the queen and the queen mother. I could never quite get this. No one dared move during the queens Christmas message, you know the one 'both my husband and I . . . .'

She left Victoria after the war with my dad a returned war vet'. He had drawn a soldier settlement block over in Western Australia where my sister and I were born. It didn't take dad long to realize that he couldn't make a go of his block by himself and so he ended up out on the Nullarbor chasing rabbits. This suited him well as he felt at ease out in the bush.

For a time my mum was working on a farm and she took care of us kids as she worked and things worked out alright. I got my hands on a bottle of kerosene and drank some so we got off to a bad start. By the time dad came to get us I had quite forgotten him and so was scared stiff of him. He had a red beard and straight black hair and he was so tall and big looking. I refused to go anywhere near him, and dad said 'that's alright she'll get used to me.' Perish the thought.

Cook was our first port of call or at least the first one I remember and dad had parked up near an old wash house which had a copper in it. For those who don't know a copper is a big old tub made of copper and sits over the top of a small fire. So you can light up the fire and boil the clothes. Nothing was clean in those days unless it was boiled.

After carrying us down there one under each arm, he lit the copper and began to soap us up. It dawned on me what he was going to do and I was filled with terror. Still not liking him or trusting him, I got the fright of my life. I thought he was going to boil us, and I distinctly remember being too afraid to scream as he lifted me up and plunked me into the water, the lovely warm water.

I still didn't trust him because what he did was, after he soaped me up he just dunked me under the water hair and all, twirled me round a bit by the hair and pulled me out! I remember so clearly though I was only three. I suppose he thought I'd forget it. My one clear thought was, had mum gone mad? Well she'd be hearing about this. I didn't go much on it, mum leaving us to the mercy of a mad man who laughed a lot.

From there we stayed out on the Nullarbor for a while before coming over to South Australia. We lived in a tent as did everyone on this particular journey and we ended up in the northern Flinders ranges. And I reckon that particular journey was the one I wrote about in 'North Bound for Glory.'

I saw my first artesian bore out there and in later years I stood guard over the place. That's another story. My mum was a good sport about most things, she didn't like to be ignored and we found that out the hard way. We were playing up the road one day when she called us back to school, we did correspondence and she taught us.

Well we decided to make out we couldn't hear her but we hadn't judged it too well. I was six, we played for a while but we didn't have a very good feeling about it so we went on home. She laid into us with a green sapling branch from a tree, had it all ready.

She had a big heart and provided you did the right thing she was a softy. We always thought we were the luckiest kids in the world with our parents.

She put up with a lot of garbage from us I mean we were difficult. Even dad felt the lash of her wrath from time to time.

I remember one time when I was about eight my sister and I had learned a particular man trap from dad and we thought it'd be a real hoot to do it to mum. We went about setting it up paying no mind to her temper, it was gunna be funny.

Of course we used string instead of wire and hoped her eyesight was as bad as we suspected. It was. We set the trap and then went back along the road to where dad had killed one of those sand pythons; you know those whoppers you get up there in Queensland and around the corner country there.

He'd caught it in a trap and when he bent down to see what he'd caught the thing was a couple of inches from his face. I'd never seen him get up off his knees so quick. Well, to get it out of the trap he had to get the twenty two out and shoot it. The poor thing was caught right at his throat if snakes have a throat. I don't know I suppose they do.

I mean this thing was both of dad's hands around and about seven feet long and I don't know what it weighed. I know it took us both an hour maybe more and five or six spells to drag it half a mile maybe less.

Anyhow when we got it back we stuck it under the chiller you know the mobile chilling unit. See the brilliant idea was to catch mum when she came down to get another jug of icy cold water. We didn't have a fridge and she got pretty hot out there.

So the trap rigged up between the two trees and the python in place to make her run we sat back rather pleased with ourselves and waited for the old girl to show up. The excitement of it all, I mean, how could we help ourselves? I mean it was dads fault really, fancy showing a pair like us how to set up a trap like that.

We waited, concealed behind a rather large bush with a roly poly (tumble weed bush) sat on the trap to keep it hidden and mum away from it. The idea was to catch her on the way back.

She came at last. Head down to keep her face out of the sun. We kept as quiet as a mouse, mum was singing as she went as usual. She side stepped the bush the plan was going well. I let out a long slow breath as she walked between the other two trees.

I darted out and removed the bush carefully. The way we had the snake under the chiller she didn't see it on her way to it but on the way back.

We heard her scream and then the jug with the ice water hit the ground. Yep, the plan was going well. Too well!

She fled passed us singing out to dad.

Of course in the real jungle the board that flew out and hit her would have had big spikes on it and pinned her to the other tree. But do you think she was at all grateful? Not her, no siree not a bit.

Well the sapling stick was applied to our backsides once again while dad ran down to investigate the crime scene. He was wide eyed with disbelief at the tale his wife told him.

He sat down under the tree and laughed till he couldn't get his breath. When he got back his eyes were full of admiration but I couldn't help but notice he turned his back on the caning we got. I mean we were screaming for mercy honestly.

All of a sudden the old girl couldn't belt us anymore for laughing. Pity she hadn't seen the bloody funny side of it before our seats were black and blue. Well some red welt marks anyway.

You know, the caning and the beltings we got never stopped us. I mean the traps we set for that poor woman and sometimes she didn't even hit us. One of the traps we set for her was right in front of the tank where she went a few times a day for water. It was the old hole in the ground trick, covered and concealed. We waited behind the laundry and down she went. When she got up she gave us a tongue lashing. She said some cruel things to, bringing our mental prowess in to question like that. Oh well!

That is all I've got to say on it for now so until we meet again . . . watch where you're walking mate, you never know. Thanks again, cheers.

# Chapter 5
## MY TRIP ACROSS THE CLAY PAN

One of the camps we lived at up in the cattle country was right next to a huge clay pan. I think we all know what a clay pan is huh. A huge patch of hard clay clear of any type of vegetation. Good for playing and riding bikes on. This particular was about the size of a football oval. Probably a bit bigger.

Well anyway there is no plumbing out there in these camps or there wasn't back then so we decided to build the little house way across this flat and hoped that most of the winds would be kind to us. The little house built we got on with life and working and such. The job of emptying the can always seemed to fall to me and my sister.

After we'd been at this camp for a couple of months we had somewhat of an unwelcome visitor. A huge beast of a bull came to stay and to make us all very nervous. He was a huge broad chested beast with big wide horns and he was wild as the hills. He was dark brown at the rump and black at the shoulders. His face was so black you could never quite see it. Never had the inclination to get close enough either!

Let me say here that we were so nervous because this was a lone bull and if there is one thing you look out for out in that country it is lone bulls. The very fact that they're alone can mean that they have been defeated or just plain kicked out of a herd. This puts them at odds with the world and often times they tend to want to take it out on someone. We've all heard the saying 'charge like wounded bulls.' Well that's where it comes from.

Our camp was on the opposite side of the clay pan to the outhouse and when we had to go it was a bit of a trek. My mother, god rest her, would get in the four wheel drive and drive across.

The fireplace, a hole in the ground with a fire in it, was right on the other edge of this clay pan. Now our fire place was everything to us, it was our kitchen, our dining room and our sitting room. We sat out there in all weathers, rain wind cold or scorching heat. We did have sense enough to make sure there was a tree nearby for when it was too hot. If it rained we put on jackets and hats.

I had taken a dislike to our new member he was big and wild and fearsome. I had not a skerrick of compassion for his loneliness or why he was alone, I wanted him gone. I was terrified of him. Why in god's name did he have to pick us to hang around? A bloomin' bull of all things wasn't natural like. But hang around he did for some weeks. I wasn't the only one who was scared of him either, my mum and some of the other campers were also very wary.

It didn't take a genius to figure out what he could do to our camp if he took it into his head to go crazy. And bulls went crazy all the time up in this country. Only about a year ago a bull had gone crazy and charged our camp. We'd all been sitting round the fire at the front of the caravan eating and talking in our kitchen come dining come living room under the stars. My brother who was just a baby at the time was asleep in his pram under the tree. It was about two o'clock in the afternoon, hottest part of the day.

It was just before time to go back to our school work, which was correspondence, when mum looked up and noticed a huge bull across the gully stamping his hooves. Pouring the dirt as they called it. She made a strange noise in her throat as she lifted her arm and pointed. We looked where she was pointing and I swear my stomach dropped.

Suddenly he let out a fearsome bellow that echoed round the valley. We knew we were in trouble. Come to think of it I could feel a trip to the toilet coming on that day to. My stomach went wild as it always did when I was scared.

'Arthur' she breathed, almost afraid the bull would hear her and take offence. He was probably half a kilometre away but we could see him quite clearly in the dimming light. He was big and white and ugly as sin.

Just then he started to pour the dirt with his front hooves and toss his head and bellow. This went on for a little while. We watched. Our old blister type caravan wouldn't even slow him down. Never the less when he put down his head and charged we all had the same idea.

To the caravan! My dad grabbed his rifle and went to stand his ground at the front of his camp and his family. He put the thing to his shoulder and took aim and waited. The bull was coming full pelt in a cloud of dust and a thunder of hooves.

In the background however, we had all forgotten Bruce in his pram and were now stuck in sort of a bottle neck at the door of the van. My mother had her foot up in the doorway but my bum was wedged firmly in the doorway with hers. Of course she won the contest, well there was no contest really, she was a very strong woman. I was eight. And she had the advantage of having her foot in the door way. But I stuck fast, motivated by terror, blind terror. That bull sounded as bad as he looked. And that was worse than mum when she was in a temper. Just.

With just a heave of her elbow I was dislodged, she got in first and I got in second, my sister came third. Bruce? Well he slept through it anyway. And Dad waited til the last minute and the bull swerved and trotted off up the road. A close call a very close call.

Now here we were this bull on our doorstep watching and waiting. For what? Waiting for me to slip up and walk passed him a bit close? Or one of the others maybe? Was that his game? Pick us off one by one? Well I intended to be careful, real careful.

We sat at the fire one night after tea, just us and the old guy from the next camp. Just sitting around the fire talking and telling stories. I was relaxed this particular night as we hadn't seen the bull for over a week. We'd had curried rabbit for tea and my stomach was letting me know about it.

'Can I take the car and go to the lav' mum?' I asked as I rose from my seat which was a four gallon drum with a bag over it. We'd been doing that a bit at night, taking the car because of that pesky bull but now that that wasn't a problem anymore we had to walk. So I walked.

Up there and back. No drama, my stomach felt better and now I was on my way back to the fire. I kept my eyes fixed on that fire. The comforting light of the fire. Something drew my eyes to the heavens and I marvelled at the night sky and the stars and the ring around the moon. Maybe rain I thought cheerfully.

I realised I wanted to get back to the fire. Quickly! For some inexplicable reason the hair on the back of my neck tickled. I could feel him. I started to walk faster, not too fast so as someone would notice but faster. I could feel him in my bones, I walked faster. The fire was only about a couple hundred yards away, I'd soon be in its comforting light.

'The bastards' back' I breathed to myself. The warm glow of the fire lost its comfort, I was in the dark. Beckoning me to safety and warmth I had the urge to run to the fire. 'Oh to hell with this,' I thought and took off. Full speed in about three steps, I ran like a frightened rabbit.

The fire light disappeared; I could see nothing and for an instant all was total darkness.

What . . . ? I started to think but got no farther when I hit something which resembled a brick wall.

When I hit it I couldn't comprehend it. I bounced off that damn bull and my feet were out from under me and I landed flat on my backside. I sat in the dirt scurrying across the ground on my behind gibbering like a fool. Though stiffening with terror I knew I should try and put some distance between us. I could not get to my feet. My heart was not in my mouth it had dropped to my rear.

I recovered somewhat comforted a little by the sound of his hoof beats disappearing into the darkness. I got to my feet, my legs shaking like jelly, and walked, I like to think, into the camp as if nothing had happened.

My mum said 'what's that?' as she looked after the noise of his retreat.

'Think it was that bull mum.' I said in a totally normal almost disinterested voice. I think.

'Damn thing I thought we'd got rid of him.' Mum said and gave me a funny look.

We never saw that old bull again, I wonder if I scared him that night. Do you like that huh, scared him? Or did he just grow tired of hanging round a bunch of human beings. Some of whom were too rude to go round an old bull standing' watching' the mesmerising flames of a campfire on a cold night in August. The strange hum of their voices the only company he had out there in the middle of nowhere. Strange things happen in the bush.

Well that's another yarn, another load off my chest. Good to know there are so many people out there willing to help, thanks again guys.

# Chapter 6

# GELIGNITE JACK

Well, Uncle Jack got a full box of gelignite and a whole roll of fuse wire and in another smaller box a whole stack of detonators. He was a funny cove and as he turned towards us his shining blue eyes gave everything away. Well this'll be good I remember thinking. I was eleven I suppose and had always loved guy forks night. I don't suppose many kids would remember guy forks night but I loved it more than I did Christmas Easter or birthdays.

My dad would nearly always come up with some fireworks for Guy Fawkes Night and us and any neighbours we might have would get out on a clay pan somewhere, light a big fire and let em off. All of us kids used to throw these little bangers at one another and make out we were having a war. It was the best fun! We all got into trouble for that incident with the penny bomber and the dogs' tail and dad told us if there was a repeat of that we'd never have guy Fawkes again. We were good! Well . . . . !

And here we were and these were real explosives, oh the fun! I looked up at him as he handled the sticks lovingly and carefully. I put my finger out hesitantly to touch one of the sticks. 'Careful' he breathed in a sort of quiet holy reverence to the sticks. They were about eight to ten inches long and were a sort of dark pink or some might say a light red in colour. Funny but they didn't look very dangerous.

Jack was a boundary rider on a dingo proof fence up in Queensland. He doubled as one of the ringers at mustering time and we'd have to go look for sheep and cattle to brand or shear depending. He'd have to go and help out at the shearing sheds to.

I loved shearing time, often we'd go and stay in the kitchen and talk with cook and wait for meal time. Contrary to popular belief, some of them cooks in the shearing sheds could bloody cook mate. A lot of times the cook would be one of the shearer's wives and they'd bring the kids along with them. We thought that was marvellous to have kids to play with.

But anyway now we had a big box of gelignite to play with and a whole stack of fuse wire the detonators and two thousand acres to play in. Some kids have all the luck I guess.

Jack had the gelignite to use whenever and wherever a job needed to be done. One of the first jobs we had to do was to bring down the old outhouse and then blow a hole for the new out house. Jack thought he needed a little practice I guess and he said we'd be going fishing.

'Before we go I might go over to the dam and throw a couple of sticks in and see how it works in the water. Do you want to come?'

Did I want to come! I nodded my head mutely and hurried out to get my boots on. I didn't bother to go back to the kitchen I thought I'd wait out the front and save time. An eternity ('bout five minutes) later Jack appeared and we were off.

We all went down to the edge of the dam that day and watched over his shoulder as he sat down on the bank of the dam and got a couple if sticks ready to throw in to the muddy water. Fascinating stuff this you know?

'Go back up to the top you'll be safe up there.' he shouted as he went to hold the match to the fuse. We ran back up onto the top of the dam to watch.

Jack had the fuse lit and he hurled the bundle into the water. Now gelignite, when you throw it in the water, bubbles. We none of us realised that it's not something you'd even think about. And all these little bubbles came up to the surface of the water as we stood there and waited for the bang.

My sister, brave little thing that she was had to be restrained as we watched her kitten cat run down to the water to play with the bubbles. Mashing, the cat stopped when she reached the edge of the water, disappointed I guess. It was only a cats' dislike of water that saved her that day.

Never the less we didn't see her for a day or so after that. When the gelignite went off with an unholy thud, a huge chute of water lifted up about ten feet into the air. It spread like a fountain and came down all over the bank of the dam where the cat was standing mesmerised by the bubbles.

All she was when she went passed us was a black streak which left behind a wet trail. She made no noise. But she came back ok a few days later on.

Now I think my sister is still a bit offended by the laughing that went on that day but it was funny. I'm not saying it would have been funny if the cat had of been hurt or something.

Anyway back to the outhouse. Jack decided we needed even more practice so we decided to go fishing in the river. We thought that there must be a huge amount of fish in there because nobody ever went there.

We packed some lunch the next day and off we went.

We decided to have a picnic lunch on the bank of this river hundreds of miles from anywhere under a beautiful big gum tree. The branches hung down almost to the ground all around and made you think you were in a room or something. And it was cool under there and the smell of eucalypt hung in the air. The cooking and the Billy we boiled outside. See? Just like a house!

We couldn't wait to try out our new style of fishing though so off we went to the water's edge. Once again Jack got the gelignite ready and threw her into the river. The fountain, the bang and then nothing. Nothing floated to the top. All except for one old snake who went passed us without even knowing we were there. He was travelling zigzag style and going pretty slow so I don't think he was a great fan of the gelignite either.

No fish! Story of my life. 'Oh you should a' been here yesterday, they were biting like mad'. Sound familiar?

Anyhow home we went disappointed but not discouraged. That outhouse was coming' down! We thought, just to be funny, we'd drop the stuff down the long drop and let her go from there. 'Should be a riot' says my uncle whom I have come to doubt in later years, as far as his mental prowess is concerned.

My aunt didn't want to go she was busy washing. There's your first clue right there. Had we connected the dots we could have saved ourselves a whole lot of grief. And grief we got when the contents of the hole under the old outhouse came down, carried by the wind, all over the washing. Anyway, I'm still here so that bears testimony to the speed in these legs of mine.

I watched from the safety of a huge peppercorn tree, believe it or not, as my uncle got aunts' bucket round his backside several times because he couldn't run seeing as he was doubled over at the time.

Now what's the moral of this story? Well I'll leave that to you, I take after my uncle you see, so be on the lookout. Cheers!

# Chapter 7

# MAYNARD, HERO EXTRAORDINAIRE

I want to tell you a story about my uncle Maynard. He was also an old army mate of dads, a man by the name of Maynard also known as the rat of IBook, war hero extraordinaire. An old World War 2 vet he'd been shot in the head in Europe and was very lucky to be alive.

The bullet had entered his forehead and exited out through the top of his head just missing vital parts. His eyes, we used to joke to him, because he didn't use his brain much anyway. He'd let out this awful roar and run after us and sometimes he caught us and stuck us up on the roof. We loved him anyway and trusted him above all others excepting our father and mother. Funnily enough!

The awful thing was he'd had to insert his finger into the wound in his forehead to stop the bleeding. When they got him to a hospital a few days later they had to perform surgery to get it out of there. So many jokes were made about this beautiful human being having his finger in his head as you can imagine and he laughed at every one of me. It was his middle (or rude) finger to.

The bullet had come from a sniper and Maynard got off a couple of shots before he went down and winged the so n so just enough to put him out of action and warn the guys coming long. The men coming along behind him thought he was dead and were shocked when Maynard got to his feet and started looking about for his rifle, cursing and swearing with blood everywhere.

He also had a huge lump on his eyebrow or at least where his eyebrow should have been. He'd apparently been driving a truck through the jungle in New Guinea when it happened.

My dad had just crossed the bridge on foot. Maynard was driving across the bridge when a grenade hit the back left hand side of the truck knocking it over the edge. The truck was leaning over the edge and didn't actually fall into the river. Maynard was slammed up against the driver side door which swung opened and he fell out and down thirty feet or so into the swirling muddy water below. His eyebrow was ripped off by the door catch on his way out. When they dragged him out of the water they thought he was dead and went back to their fighting and left him there for later.

That night as they were bedding down on the ground, or should I say collapsing where they stood exhausted and hurt, some dead, from all that days fighting, Maynard staggered into camp with ashen face and staring eyes. And he made some of them believe in ghosts. I can understand that to because Maynard had jet black hair and thick black eyebrow or at least one thick black eyebrow. There was a lot of blood and he looked to have an eye missing.

He was laughing crazily and not making much sense. He gabbled something about the japs getting a little surprise and the men put it down to the shock. Dad laid his best mate gently on the ground and flopped down himself, too exhausted to speak.

Later that night as they all slept there was an unholy bang that seemed to split the night in two. The earth moved and the bridge came down and took with it all the Japanese soldiers who were guarding it. Every last one of 'me apparently.

Those soldiers, who still could, jumped to their feet, guns ready. No one spoke as they began to crouch down on the ground. The smoke in the air was suffocating.

'They won't catch us in a hurry now hay mate' laughed Maynard to my father and passed out in his arms.

Dad laughed. 'You set a trap for 'em Maynard?' he whispered surprised but Maynard was already out to it.

Once again he got carted off to hospital this time it took a lot longer than a few days and so Maynard was stuck forever with a huge lump on his brow. He looked quite comical.

But my uncle Maynard and all of the other uncles I had, home from the war, never got over it. Of all the heroes I grew up with, he was my favorite. He was gentle and kind and loving mostly and he always brought us treats. Lollies, biscuits, fruit and drinks. Of course he laughed and joked a lot to.

Sometimes I would see him laughing but different, and he'd laugh again and again until the tears rolled down his cheeks, the tears he couldn't stop. And he would just withdraw. Where he went I do not know but the pain and the horror on his face told me it must have been some where pretty terrible.

On these occasions the only thing I could do was to wait quietly and my heart broke a little with every tear. My dad was the same and so I knew how to sit quietly and wait from when I was very young. Somehow I could feel their pain but I couldn't help them.

And my dear old uncle Maynard had gotten a Dear John letter from his sweetheart just before he was de mobbed and never got over that either. We were the only family he had in the world and we considered it an honour and today I still remember him as my uncle Maynard.

I remember once when he came to visit he brought with him an old car, I think it was an old T model ford. He handed my sister and I all these little cans of paint and told us he wanted it painted all colours. We couldn't believe our luck!

Sometimes my uncle Maynard went mad and did things that were completely out of character. One time the boss' truck wouldn't start so Maynard got his gun and filled it full of holes. I think he got the sack.

He had an old blue heeler dog called Bluey and that dog went everywhere with him. Maynard always boasted he had the smartest dog in the world and that may be true.

One day as he was driving along he hit a kangaroo, something he would rather not have done I know. Any way he stopped and looked back and the roo never got up. He couldn't just leave it there to suffer so he grabbed a tyre lever and walked back to see if the animal was dead or alive or hurt.

Well this big old red kangaroo got up and chased him scratching him down the back until his shirt was in tatters and all bloody. It chased him round and round the car until Maynard got far enough in front to jump in and slam the door shut. The old Kangaroo banged on the window which Maynard just wound up in time and hopped away. Vindicated.

Maynard turned around and thanked his very smart dog for not doing a thing to help him. Bluey knew not to mess with kangaroos lest they mess with you. So maybe he really was the smartest dog in the world.

He upset my mum from time to time to. He was leaving our house one day, I remember it was the very first house I'd lived in, I was ten. He'd borrowed dad's trailer for some reason. I stood waving him off with mum when he got the trailer caught on the fence. Mum sang out to him to stop.

He stopped and got out of the car and walked back to inspect it. He turned around and walked back to the car muttering something as he went. I couldn't believe my ears as I sucked in air. Oh this was gunna be good!

Mum whispered 'I didn't think he was going to stop there for a minute.' I glanced up at her relieved expression. Shit I thought as I turned my grinning face away from her.

Maynard slammed the car door and puts it in to gear. I held my breath I really did. He tramped his foot and away he went taking most of the back fence with him. The neighbours, gawping over the fence as usual, eyes wide like saucers, weren't too delighted, as half of their back fence went to.

Maynard put his head out of the car window and sang out 'see ya toots' to my mum. There was back fence strewn along the road for miles. My heart swelled with pride, my mother hurried indoors.

I suppose I had this sort of hero worship going on with my uncle Maynard, I mean the man taught me how to play cards for god's sake. I know when he left I was sad 'til he came back.

Many years later I got into trouble playing cards because I should have been voting at the time. I wriggled out of it I'd rather not say how. That's another story as they say; one day I might tell it who knows.

These old diggers were a breed apart and sometimes it was hard to imagine they'd ever been anything else. Hard to imagine that once they'd been young boys with the same hopes and dreams as any other boy. They were heroes true, but they were hurt in such a way as cannot be fixed. At least not at the present time. I mean, how do you put the dreams back into someone who's been to hell? Someone who's broken like that?

And today, my Roly, the love of my life who brings me such joy has been to the same place and I am powerless to help him either. So I can only go on waiting quietly and patiently while he goes to a place I don't know about and he can't tell me about. The same place as made those strong men, those heroes like my dad and uncle Maynard, weep.

How do I put the dreams back in him? After he has known a horror and fear that we could never imagine, and has had to take part in that horror and death and destruction.

The never to be forgotten sights and sounds and smells and even the taste of war and death and blood. Of smoke and explosives and to feel the earth move with every explosion. Has had to face his own death. Not only somebody else's, his. And faced it time and time again. Every time they marched into battle with their company they were dead men walking. How many times can you die and still be the same? They all deserve their hero status as far as I am concerned.

Well anyway for now these men have, or should bloody well have, a nation of people who are eternally grateful. This is their story and I take my hat off to you brave men who laid your life down for us over and over again. And if I may; I salute you all.

# Chapter 8

# AN ORANGE TREE GROWS

I shall always remember this old orange tree as long as I live. An old orange tree it was and it had me stumped. See I always prided myself in the fact that I could get in anywhere and help myself to various fruits in any backyard in any town.

No fruit tree, vine or bush was safe as long as I, Mary Seaton, was around Just in and out and no one any the wiser. But not this orange tree, I mean I spent hours sitting on this fence trying to think of a way passed this savage bloody dog underneath it.

It had become a matter of personal pride. Not to mention those lovely oranges just going to waste. If I had gone and asked I would have got some probably but then if Dad found out I'd asked I'd have got somewhat of a bollickin' if I was lucky.

I even got into Wally Sheeman's back yard and he was a brute of a man and hated us kids. He was always on the lookout for us and ranting and raving about what he would do to us 'little mongrels' If he caught us.

Well he didn't catch me and I sat under his grapevine eating his grapes watching him walk up and down loading his Ute up to go to Broken Hill. He would have been about ten feet away. I could've reached out and handed him one of his own grapes.

Every yard in that town had a grape vine we had two in ours, but it was a matter of personal pride like I said. I was somewhat of a hero for a while, what is it they say? 'I was a legend in my own mind'.

Well anyway this dog was a very nasty cove and very well fed to, I found that out the hard way. I think he only feigned an interest in the chop bone I threw him so's I'd make the mistake of jumping in his yard. He bloody nearly got me to I was over that fence and out like a rat up a drain pipe. His teeth buried into my pants and ripped 'em. Mum went crook at me for being a tear coat but she didn't ask.

I wasn't beaten yet, not until the last orange dropped off that bloomin' Tree. Anyhow, nor was he interested in the mouse I dropped in there or the dead bird or the sheep's head. I even threw in a dead dog that had been run over on the road. But that gave me an idea.

It was sheer bloody brilliance I only wished I could tell somebody! Of course I didn't, I was smart enough even at eleven to keep the old trap shut.

I might add though that I have even seen this trick done in a movie in recent years but I think it worked a bit better in the movie. Well doesn't it always?

Over the railway line mum had become friends with these people who shall remain nameless. They were peculiar people, slow. Well more backwards I think, probably a bit retarded. Well very retarded actually the father had a few 'roos loose in the top paddock but the mother had a whole trainload.

The kids were my biggest annoyance wanting to know what I was doing all the time. They'd follow me for god's sake asking me dumb questions. I was a solitary person, I operated alone. Unless of course I needed an audience.

I didn't get on too well with the other girls in this particular place but that didn't worry me much we weren't gunna be staying long thank God and then we'd be off back to the sand hills and Queensland.

I remember this one time though; I took my little brother, who would have been three at the time to the park. It was a nice day and he was enjoying it immensely on the swings and that and so was I. Just my little brother Bruce and me.

But they couldn't just leave us alone you know. Pretty soon all these kids came out of nowhere and they were carrying a bucket which they were trying to conceal behind their back. Well you guessed it they had all these little baby paddy melons in it which they started throwing at us. They really hurt to. They splatter when they hit and sting.

Any how I picked my baby brother up and ran. It hurt the old pride more than anything but I couldn't do anything else with a baby to look after. That's right, look after! I held him close in front of me as I ran so as none would hit him. But even in my dilemma I marked every one of their laughing triumphant faces for the day of reckoning.

One by one I got everyone of 'em and taught 'em a couple of lessons. One, the difference between acting in a pack and going it alone. Not so big when they faced me one on one. And two I taught the boys that it wasn't always a good idea to mindlessly do as the girls told em. After that I pretty much did what I liked and nobody opposed me. All except this ruddy dog.

I was sitting, studying the problem one day when these little kids that I told you about came over to start bugging me. I was wondering whether throwing a poor dead dog in there was a bit over the top. Nah I says to myself.

'Is your mum n dad takin one of our pups?' the little boy says.

'What pups?' I asked disinterestedly.

'The ones our dogs havin you know.'

'Is she preggas?' I asked. 'You know has she got puppies in her belly?'

'Not yet but she's on heat and dad put another dog in with her . . . .'

Well that's disgusting from a little kids mouth I thought.

'Move along Stubby and take your pets with you.' I said indicating his little sister.

I went back to thinking but not for long. 'Shit!' I said out loud and swung round to where the little boy was walking off with his sister. I had to get my hands on that dog. 'Oy' I sang out 'do these dogs bite?'

'No' says the little boy looking all disappointed again. He turned to go.

'You can hang about for a while if you want.' I was bloody sorry as soon as I'd said it. I was somewhat of a loner see.

They ran back and I felt a bit bad, just a bit for what I was about to do.

'I saw your mother going home from the shop with a big bag of lollies' I said and felt not a jot of compassion for their pending disappointment as they raced off and left me to my thoughts. My plans.

Now getting hold of this bitch was easy, the bloody thing was always getting out. The people were not very bright as I have said. I got hold of her as the light was fading into darkness the following day. She vaguely knew me and came to me when I called to her softly.

With no thoughts of any other possible outcomes but the one I had planned I tossed the little bitch over the fence.

The bully ran after her as planned. I jumped the fence as planned. I got two huge oranges as planned but I never ate them. Technically I did get the oranges but I didn't have em long enough to eat em so you be the judge as to whether I won or lost.

My parents had left a certain operation out of my education see. First blood to the dog. No one ever figured out how the little bitch got in the yard with the orange tree either. No one ever pinned it on me, on that Seaton girl. Too slick for that mate.

The oranges went on withering and rotting on the ground under the tree a terrible waste I thought. My reputation had taken a bit of a battering thanks to that cantankerous bloomin' dog.

Well anyway that's life aint it you win a few you lose a few. I left the old dog alone after that, you know, I figured he'd had enough! Ha ha ha bloody ha ha ha.

Till the next time and we'll tell a few more tales in the shade hay, see ya down the track mate stay well.

# Chapter 9

# A WALK IN THE DESERT

Well here I was on my way to get water one job I didn't mind doing. I was twelve and I loved driving. Later in life I became a Truckee but that's got very little to do with this story. We had to cart our water up there, take forty four gallon drums to the bore and fill them with water and cart it home see.

Now this water we used for everything and we used it very carefully. We also drank this water and every time we shifted camp we had to drink different water from a different bore. This lead to a good old dose of the runs every time we shifted.

I had just two drums to fill and so I swung the pipe that went from the windmill to the tank over to the drums and hooked up the hose. The drums were full in no time and so I hopped back in the Toyota to head home. Quite pleased I might add and relieved to have beaten the very large herd of very wild cattle on their way in to drink.

Even as far away as they were I could just make out some very large beasts out in front. Wild, scrubber bulls. Enough to send a chill down your spine just thinking about em. Now these critters get mighty ornery when they are hot and thirsty and they don't take kindly to anyone getting in their way. Well I planned on getting right out of their way. Soon!

And it was hot today must have been forty in the shade at least. Not that there was much of that around. Just the odd scraggy little mulger tree I noticed as I looked over to where the herd was raising quite a dust cloud as they came.

'Must be coming fast' I mused as I swung my leg up into the four wheel drive.

Cattle tend to stampede when they get the smell of water in their nostrils and on a day like today I didn't blame them. As the summer progressed and still no rains to bring up the summer grasses, they had to travel farther and farther from their only water supply to get feed.' Poor beggars' I mused again as I reached down to turn the key to start the motor up. Yep, wouldn't want to get in their way, sure makes you appreciate the old four wheel drive mate I thought as I turned the key. And you know that old Toyota decided she wasn't going anywhere and neither was I. And that huge dust cloud scattered right across the horizon, well that was between me and home.

'Wonderful' I murmured as I put my head on my arm to wipe the sweat from my eyes, 'just bloody wonderful.' I glanced down at the seat on my left and put my hand down to touch the comforting smooth butt of my trusty twenty two. A Brno it was with telescopic sights, lovely piece of work. You couldn't miss.

It was around ten miles home so I thought I'd best get walking. I knew what was wrong with the bloody Toyota but I didn't have the tools to fix it. Ok so I was twelve alright? And I am female and we seldom bother ourselves with such things.

Any hoot I grabbed up the rifle to get a better look through the sights at what was coming fast toward me and immediately wished that I hadn't.

It was very a large herd with all manner of beasts. Some of last year's progeny had made it, almost, to full growth and had grown into some quite good looking beasts. But not today. Some of this year's progeny were still hangin with their mothers and that was double trouble. Some of those old cows could get very nasty if they thought you were trying mess with their young. And who in their right mind would want to mess with junior?

Anyway, I'm sure you can understand why I made the decision to take the rifle with me even though it was heavy and put a limit on how much water I could carry. I just wasn't very strong see, but sort of on the puny side. I was very fast, but not strong.

I reckoned it'd be about half passed two so the hottest part of the day was all but. So off I went hoping to skirt the herd and avoid any con—frontations which could get ugly and not necessarily in favour of yours truly.

Just like my father before me and in the tradition of the great Seaton Clan, I kicked the bloody Toyota in the guts, swore at it and left it standing there on the bank of the dam. With a bit of a limp, rifle over one shoulder, water bag over the other and my hat pulled down low over my eyes I set forth on my journey home.

I was in good spirits despite my concerns about the cattle. I hadn't gone a mile when I needed a good swig of water. The rifle was getting heavy, I was getting thirsty and I began to doubt my decision to carry less water. However as I was in the process of dodging cattle my mind was mostly, otherwise occupied. The trees were a little thicker here and with the dust, cut visibility down some.

I'd skirted the main herd but I was on the lookout for the stragglers and there were plenty of em. Luckily they were for the most part too thirsty to be inclined to want to pay much attention to me. That is until I met a very large and very angry bull who, I would say had just been ousted from the family. They are mean when in this state! He looked like the devil himself, a very big hairy devil.

Well I won't bore you with the details, he just charged me. Didn't even think about it he just full on charged me. Put his head down and came at me full pelt from a few hundred meters. Not far, not nearly far enough.

No problems, I had the rifle and I could shoot as straight and fast as anybody can, just like Johnny. It's just that I had the magazine in my pocket. So I had to turn and run. Fast! I looked for a big tree and there were none, nothing high enough to escape the big boy behind me who, although I could run like the wind, was closing fast. Not a fence anywhere in sight, nothing.

I slid the rifle off my shoulder into my left hand and the water bag I dropped in the dirt. As I'm running I'm trying to get the blasted magazine out of the pocket of my jeans which had been selected for having pockets that things didn't come out of too easy. Ten out of ten to those pockets! So with my hand full of thumbs I managed to get the magazine out of my pocket. That magazine felt good in my palm, real good.

Now I can tell by the noise behind me that I don't have time to load so I turned and faced him. He was about a hundred yards away now. I yelled at him and ran at him. He was surprised and slowed down but he kept coming.

By now I've got the magazine in my right hand, rifle in my left but I can't afford to take my eyes off the bull. He could kill me with just one blow from those huge horns. Talk about David and Goliath but I had Mr. Equalizer in my hands! I just had to load it.

Ten yards between us and I stopped and threw myself to the side and quickly rolled to my knees and to my feet and ran the other way to give me some time, even a couple of seconds would come in handy. I felt the magazine slip nicely into the gun and I hammered the bolt home just as I turned back to face the bull.

The bull slows up to turn realizing that he's been duped and I'm back there somewhere, they're not the brightest animal on earth. You don't really need to be when you're that big. But now I've got a bullet in the breach. I put the rifle to my shoulder tucked in nice and snug. My knees are shaking like a bastard but I figure I can still hit him in the head which must have been about two feet across. Almost point blank mate he's gunna drop aint he.

He lowered his head to charge, fifty to a hundred yards between us. Not far. Suddenly I lost his head from my sights and for an instant I felt the panic in the pit of my belly.

I lifted my head and opened both my eyes for a better look; he'd thrown his head back. The mongrel of a thing has called off the charge; he turned around and ran off! The smell of water must have got up his nostrils and he couldn't resist.

I watched him go, he looked back at me once and he was gone. 'Thank god for that' I said out loud as my legs gave out from under me.

Jesus I needed a drink about now I picked up the water bag and lifted it to my mouth and drank heavily from it. Now I had even less water but I didn't want to meet him again so I got up and made for home. I might add, on the shakiest pins I've ever had beneath me.

I must have been walking for an hour and a half maybe two when I took another swig from the water bag and figured that I probably had another two swigs left maybe three. I had drunk most of my water. I guessed that I'd have about two, maybe three miles to go.

After I'd walked another hour I stopped and took the last swig. The sun was getting low on the horizon but the heat was not easing off. I dropped the water bag on the ground and leaned the gun up against a tree. I still thought I'd make it ok though.

On and on I trudged in the stifling heat, my mouth was dry and it felt like it was burning. I started to hum a tune but kept forgetting what I was humming. Had to try and keep my mouth closed. Losing too much moisture. Had to walk steady and try to keep the sweat down to a minimum. My throat was dry to and it hurt to swallow. And funnily enough, I kept trying to swallow.

I kept on; I figured I had about a mile to go now. My tongue was swelling and breathing was a bit labored. The sun still had a sting in it and the hot north wind was baking my skin. I was very fair. It felt like I was burning and my clothes felt like they were rubbing the skin right off me. I had to keep telling myself that I must leave them on and not take them off.

My head had started pounding and I started to feel sick. Dehydration had set in. Then, at last, I had reached the top of the last hill and there, down in the valley I saw the caravan, the tent and the smoke from the fire. Home! Everything I loved, just down there. Almost a half a mile away. I whistled as loud as I could in the hopes that one of the dogs would hear me. You try whistling with dry parched lips that were cracked and bleeding. Not easy huh. If I'd only kept the gun,

All I could do was put my head down and trudge on, one foot in front of the other. My head pounding I started to feel light headed. It got so bad I thought I was going to faint. Keep going I told myself. My body started to feel too heavy for my legs to carry and I found myself lying face down in the dirt. And this is after just a few hours in the sun without water.

As soon as I had got off my feet the cramps hit, first in the feet and then up the backs of my legs. All I could do was groan until it passed. Jesus it hurt, I limped for days after. I turned my face towards home. I couldn't believe I was going to die here so close to home. My stomach heaved a couple of times and settled back down. I raised my eyes to the sky, it was sun down. It would soon be dark.

My head was pounding so bad that I closed my eyes against it. When it had passed a little I opened them and for the second time that day was frightened almost to death by a strange looking animal. I tried to get my eyes focused but before I could I'd copped a sloppy lick right up the length of my face. I raised my hand weakly and then let it fall back down. The fright had robbed me of very valuable strength.

It was Butch the cattle dog, come to save me. I tried to sit up but he was right in front of me. He licked my face again and again and again. Well at least my face was wet anyhow.

'Good boy Butch' I said, 'go and get dad.' I said it again 'go and get dad.' But alas he was not Skippy. But he was very excited now and he stood on my hair and my arms and then he tripped on my sore leg and then stood on my sore foot. Now he was licking my arms. He was a big solid dog and every time he stepped on my sunburned limbs he was takin skin off!

'Butch!' I tried to shout, 'go fetch dad Butch. Go on fetch dad! **F-e-t-c-h d-a-d!**'

The confused dog ran off and picked up a big stick, more like a tree stump really, brought it back and dropped it in my face. I let out a yell and the dog licked my arm. 'Now my face will have scars' I whinged. I started wishing I had never bloody whistled him.

I struggled up into a sitting position hoping to ward off any more good intentions and down the road I saw dad and Ray coming. They were coming fast like the devil was after em. 'Oh good' I looked at the dog 'now I'm gunna get run over.'

However, they did spot me and skidded to a halt and sat there looking at me over the bonnet. I must have looked quite a sight! Ray pulled the Toyota up beside me and dad looks at me from the window and says 'Jesus you look a mess. Broke down did ya? Why didn't you wait? You knew I'd come lookin for ya. Why did you walk home? Shit we better get you home to your mother.'

'Just give me the water and take that bloody dog' I sort of croaked. Dads' mouth was hanging opened.

He shoves his big hand out the window and I grabbed the water bag out of it. I guzzled. Cool life giving water, truly the nectar of the gods.

Dad got out of the vehicle and snatched the water bag off me. 'Here, here take it easy with that.' He said. 'Jesus you are a mess. Look at your poor little face! Ya poor little bugger'

I snatched the water bag back and as he helped me up out of the dirt and into the front seat I says 'if you're going to get the Toyota I hope you've got your tools with you.' I felt the gleam in my eye as his face told me he didn't.

'Come on kid we'll get you home first.' He got up in the back and whistled that bloody dog up with him. Of course a couple of hours later I was best mates with the dog again.

At home my mother was horrified at the sight of me. 'What happened?' she asked as I sank down on my bed and there I slept till next afternoon.

I was very careful what I told them and went off to look in the mirror to see what people were staring at. I knew it was bad but shit I looked a fright. Two big blisters that looked like bags of water hung from either side of my face. 'No wonder I was bloody thirsty' I said quietly as I nodded at my reflection. My lips were swollen and cracked and I had a giant scratch down my nose and chin where the dog had dropped the tree on it. But I was live wasn't I?

That night around the camp fire with all our neighbours, come to have a look, while we waited for the Billy to boil I was the entertainment. Now they say that laughter is the best medicine and that my friends is probably why I got better so quick! And no scars, nary a one!

Well anyway, till we meet again, remember what I always say and look out for lone bulls mate no matter where you are. One thing I did learn was that if you are gunna carry a gun to protect yourself you may as well have it loaded. What say you? Adios.

# Chapter 10

# THE BROLGAS DANCED

I want to tell this story about a not so well known bird as the emu but an Australian feathered resident just the same. I believe they rate a mention as one of the most talented and beautiful birds in this country. These birds like to live deep in the outback away from civilization as far as they can get.

The day was a scorcher, the road just a dusty track snaking and winding its way into the never never. Here and there along the track were potholes of bull dust you could just about disappear into and not be seen again. A little bit of bush humour there.

To the north and to the south of us the heat shimmers danced about on the top of the ranges as we travelled along the valley in between. We had entered South Australia about five hours ago on our way to Mare. Dad wanted to catch up with a rabbit buyer there.

My early years with my parents were spent chasing rabbits about the country. We had lived in all the mainland states by the time we went to school.

Most of our schooling was done by correspondence. I remember my first teacher was a Miss Fox in Adelaide South Australia. Incidentally she was the first person who got me interested in writing and drawing.

I looked about me as I stood up to walk back to the car. I had just been sick for the umpteenth time and my head ached and throbbed. I shut the car door behind me and lay down on the seat to pass out again.

It was March 1962 just a few months from my eighth birthday and I had some sort of tummy upset. The flies were awfully sticky and the air was thick, a sure sign of rain coming. Dad was a bit worried and wanted to get as far as we could before dark.

The next thing I was aware of was dad's voice saying 'come on kid you have to eat something. Here come on up you come' he hoisted me up off the seat.

We were pulled up under a tin shed to shelter for the night out of the rain. I protested but mum shoved some tinned pineapple in my mouth and it didn't taste half bad, so I ate.

Then in to my little swag and off to sleep, glorious sleep. The last thing I remembered was the sound of gentle rain beating softly on the tin roof. Perfect.

Next day I felt much better but my head still ached a little so I spent most of the day sprawled out in the back seat. We had passed from rocky hilly country to sand hill country and I hadn't noticed. But at least I wasn't sick anymore. I loved the sand hills; they seemed so much softer than rocks and stone of the ranges country.

I came to with a start. My mother was shaking me awake and as I opened my eyes she held her finger to her lips for me to be quiet. 'Ssh, brolgas.' She whispered, her eyes wide with excitement, 'sit up and be quiet and if we are very luck they might dance for us.'

I knew from the way she spoke that we were about to see something very special. I looked out the window and down to where the brolgas stood looking back at us. Two of them, beautiful birds. Long graceful legs and neck. They were bluey grey with red caps on the tops of their heads.

We sat in silence, not bothering to try and hide, 'they like to show off" said mum. They stood looking from us to each other and back again. My headache was forgotten in anticipation, I was just about bursting.

The brolgas faced each other and after the longest pause ever they danced. There on a clay pan in the red sand, the sky a deep blue amongst the green spinifex and wild flowers freshened by the rain and small pools of water I saw my very first dance show. A beautiful graceful dance of two of the most beautiful birds I've ever seen against the splendour and majesty of the Australian outback. My headache was gone.

Years later and hundreds of miles from that spot I witnessed this dance once more. Two brolgas stopped by at our damn near our house to drink. Mum spotted them and alerted the rest of the family.

We lined up on the front veranda to wait. The place was Bindarah gate on the dingo proof fence on the border of N.S.W. and QLD. We were right in the middle of the channel country and when the Bulloo River up north burst its banks we would be surrounded by flood waters, cut off from everywhere.

The wild life that came down with the floods was amazing. The empty sand hill country would suddenly be teaming with all manner of wildlife. Birds and animals and insects of all shapes and sizes and glorious colours to.

One of my favourites was the black swan. The humble frog who, as a magician has my utmost resects, springs to life just minutes after the water descends. He makes up for years of silence I can tell you.

We waited in silence, anticipating a good show there on the red bank of the damn which reared up from the green, grey vegetation of the channel country. The deep blue of the sky and the fluffy white clouds made a wonderful back drop. One of nature's most dramatic stages set for two of nature's most wonderful dancers

We waited, not game to move as the minutes ticked by. The two birds, they are usually in twos, looked back at us in silence. Then they turned to each other and dipped. We knew it was Showtime!

There from the veranda of our humble abode we watched a dance show fit for a king. They swayed their long necks and slender bodies to an ancient rhythm and dipped their legs and stepped to a beat all their own. And they never missed a beat as they sallied round one another, dipping and swaying, this way and that. Turning and strutting, leading and following they danced.

It was beautiful. I have seen dance shows since in the finest of places, from tap to ballet, ballroom to cabaret but nothing quite compares to the lovely Aussy brolga.

All too soon it was over. They looked back towards us and turned about. As they walked down the bank and out of sight I whispered to them to come back. How I wanted those birds to stay and I prayed that they would but they had to be free to roam just like we did.

I have never seen one in captivity and nor would I want to. For if they were locked up they would lose their magic. And what if the brolga should forget how to dance?

I pray for a lot of things I know but I do pray for the brolgas that they will remain safe in their habitat, the Australian outback for years to come. And I pray that they will still be dancing for our children's children for I am sure they will love them as I do.

# Chapter 11

# WHILE DINGOES HOWLED ALL AROUND

Every week or so my dad would take a break from shooting so he could get a good night's sleep. On these occasions my sister and I could take the four wheel drive and the rifle and go get us some rabbits and make some money. Only way for us to get money in those days was to go earn it. If somebody had suggested to my parents that they give us an allowance they would have got a good old belly laugh out of that. I can just see dad's face.

In this particular camp there were four families. I think we all thought we were in some kind of wagon train because our camps or communes if you like were usually all in a circle. I was aged just thirteen when I first came in gun shooter for the night I'd gotten the most rabbits and all head shot. You could still get money for em if they were shoulder shot but only half as much. If dad had of been out that night I wouldn't have, jeez that man could shoot. If he aimed at something he got it.

One night in the mid-autumn weeks of that year which was '67 I reckon, my sister and I were preparing to go out shooting. We were shooting rabbits which were kept cold in a chiller (mobile chilling unit), gutted but not skinned.

Every few months or so the old blitz came up from Yunta mostly to bring us stores and take the rabbits away. These rabbits were carted to Melbourne I think and then sold to Japan and other countries outside of Australia and I think we were getting about eighty cents a pair. Rabbits were big business then.

In earlier years my dad trapped them a practice which was banned in later years, recognized for the cruel practice that it was. Thank god for small mercies ay.

Well anyway as he went round his traps he'd get the rabbits out of the traps and kill them and put them in a sack on his back. And every half hour he would gut them else they'd go off.

Someone once told him he should carry them in the sack alive as then you don't have to clean so often. One night he decided to give this a go. I shall never forget the look on his face when he emptied that bag out on the ground as per his usual and rabbits went everywhere. They scattered in all directions and when dad got over his shock he looked at me and laughed. 'Bugger that' he says 'we'll do it my way.'

Back to the story, we had everything ready and the sun was setting fast and mum called out did we want to take some food.

'No' we says 'we won't be stopping tonight thanks mum.'

'Well' she says 'you want to take something warm, you know, just in case.'

'Yes mum we've got all that. We've got everything we need we are not babies.' I was cocky and no one could tell me when I thought I knew. I wanted to get going. Rabbits to shoot and money to be made.

'Alright' she says 'be careful out there.'

I slipped the old Toyota into gear and tramped my foot and we were off. Off to make some money, I loved that idea and I loved being out there amongst it. I had no desire to live in a nice warm house in nice crowded suburbia. No siree, not this little black duck.

We had been at it for a few hours and probably around eleven or twelve o'clock we stopped I think for the third time to clean.

About half an hour before this we had ran into a patch of dingoes so we tried to bag us one of them with no luck. There was quite a bounty on them in those days I just forget how much. We singled one out and chased him for about fifteen minutes and I nearly rolled the Toyota on a spinifex bush. So we left the dingoes in peace and went on our way cruising and looking for rabbits.

Back to the cleaning, the night was very cold and so we set fire to a spinifex bush to keep warm. I tell you what those bushes burned big and gave out tremendous heat and light but they didn't last very long. When the cleaning was done we jumped back in the old girl to get started. The old girl had other ideas and she just wouldn't start. We tried everything we knew and still no go. It was cold and we climbed despondently back in the cabin.

I looked at Jude and she looked at me and we both looked out at the clear freezing night. With no doors on the Toyota we'd have to come up with something to keep us warm. We had brought no blankets tarps or anything else like that. We had taken no notice of mother.

We went off to search for wood she went one way, and I another. The night was so clear and the moonlight so bright we didn't take long to find enough wood for the night. We got a fire started and Jude started skinning a rabbit we were starving now.

While she was doing this I sat looking despairingly into the flames. My mind returned to the patch of dingoes we had chased and whether or not they bore us any ill will. My sister told me not to chase em. Shit!

'What you doin?' I asked as she went to throw some rabbit on the coals. 'Don't do that' I says 'put it in a pot and boil it. I'm not eating rabbit covered in bloody dirt n ash n shit.'

'Well OK' she says 'but we don't have any salt. It'll taste like shit.'

I looked at her, 'fine' she says and put it in a pot of water and boiled it. I couldn't eat it! She couldn't eat it. It was awful.

'Why did you boil it' I says in a huff, 'you knew it would taste like this.'

'Goodnight' she says as she lies down on the ground between the fire and the Toyota and pulls her jacket around her.

I went over to the Toyota and grabbed up the twenty two and lay down on the ground myself on the far side of the fire and away from the Toyota with its no doors. I put my arms around that rifle and hugged it to me. Bloody dingoes weren't goin to sneak up on this little black duck.

I dozed for a while I guess and then I froze, this time from the inside out. A dingo howled somewhere very close to me; I could hear him walking around. I reached down very quietly and put a bullet in the breach and neutralized the safety.

Another howl this one away a bit but on the other side. I lay still listening to my sisters steady breathing unaware we were about to die.

Another howl and another and another. There is nothing more eerie or mournful than a dingoes howl and it makes the hair stand up on the back of your neck. What I'd give for a couple of doors.

'Shit' I breathed as I sat up. I crawled around the fire and sat beside my sleeping sister my back leaning against the vehicle. She woke up.

'What's wrong?' she asked noticing my terrified expression.

'Bloody dingoes all around us' I whispered. My mouth was dry as a bone.

'So?'

'So I think they're bloody hungry' I hissed at her.

'Oh so what' she says and goes back to sleep. Back to sleep!

I must have dozed off and when I came to again I jumped. Something was wrong. Something wrong with the horizon I thought. I peered into the night. There isn't one.

'Holy cow' I screeched at Jude who came to. 'They've got us surrounded.' I let off a couple of shots just to sort em out a bit. Something strange happened, the night seemed to split in two and take off in different directions in a sound of thundering hooves.

My sister says 'You couldn't even hit a bullock. Maybe that would taste nice boiled in a pot.'

'Bloody sarcasm' I grumbled as I settled back down to keep watch for dingoes in my sleep. None came I don't think and in the morning of the next day we were rescued. Good old dad, he always came for us. He always seemed to know where we were to I'll be blowed if I know how.

# Chapter 12

# ONCE A SMOKER

I would like to tell you a story about my smoking career; however I do not intend to preach in any way shape or form. I did enjoy my smoking, a little too much I fear, and it did make me sick in the end. I hung in there though, didn't give in easily and my knocking off the smokes was just plain ugly. With the aid of sleeping pills I slept the first four days, but that's enough of that lets go back to where it all began.

When I was eight I learnt to smoke. That I learned it from my sister is incidental and I wish to make it known right here and now that I do not hold her responsible in any way shape or form. She had no choice but to share her smokes with me after all I had threatened to do on her if she refused.

'Right' I'd say, 'just wait 'til I tell mum you've been smoking.' So I got my smoke and a bit of a poke in the face to go with it sometimes. I understood later how annoying it can be because my little brother did the same to me. Blackmail starts young; in fact I think it may even be an instinct. In our family anyway.

Then one day Bruce got greedy and asked for a smoke for his three little buddies as well and that's when I decided to cut him loose. He squawked for a while about telling on me, the smoking and the poke in the face, as he picked himself up out of the dirt.

Well I reminded him, in a big sister sort of a way, that he was here asking for the bloody things himself and had been doing so for a while. And maybe, just maybe, she'd have him for smoking to. He looked abashed at his mates, who were standing staring wide eyed at me and went off mumbling and grumbling. I gave his little mates the sign and they took off to.

Anyhow, back to the story. We started off smoking rolled up newspapers and then we put dry grass in newspaper and then graduated to buts. We'd get buts and tear them open and roll the tobacco into smokes with some cigarette papers we'd stolen. Such an ugly word isn't it stolen? Helped ourselves! Well anyway we were on our way and I would say hooked like a witch's snout even then.

I think the hardest part of smoking rollies was the nicotine stains on the fingers. A dead giveaway and yet I never got caught that way. I can remember putting paint all over my fingers to try to cover it up. We tried getting it off with turps and metho' and all sorts but nothing worked.

One day when I was nine we swiped, not stole, a tin of tobacco from dad's store. We took it and some matches and papers and hid it in a hole behind a bush about two hundred yards from the caravan. Every night after tea we'd go down and get it and head for the sand hill for a smoke or two. This bush was in full view of the window at the back of the caravan.

How he found our stash I'll never know! Huh.

At the time I didn't want to know, but it doesn't take a genius. But find it he did and we got dragged in to take our punishment in front of mum dad and a mate of dads. We filed into the caravan and sat down in silence, heads hung low. 'Right' said dad, as he handed us a smoke each. 'You have to smoke these and you have to smoke it all'.

He sat back to watch the fun. I looked at him with my mouth hung open. I couldn't believe my luck, a whole smoke and we didn't have to hide away to smoke it. I threw a quick look at my sister and was so disappointed to see she wasn't enjoying it much. Dad threw us the matches and we lit up.

As I sat there puffing away my mum told us to do the draw back and so I obliged. She was shocked to see how well I did, no coughing no choking

Nothing. 'They've been at it for months' she said in shock. Best smoke I ever had.

We got our smokes smoked and were sent from my mother's sight because she didn't want to see us again that day she said. I left the camp with a heavy heart and dad's parting words of 'a lovely pair to be taking down to civilisation smoking like old men' ringing in our ears As I was going however I glanced across at the little bush and the empty hole behind it and vowed and declared that I would be a bit smarter next time. Wouldn't be too hard huh? Never again would they catch me smoking. It wasn't long until my brother stumbled across my nasty habit and made his move. When he was about five he was always going on about how he was going to smoke cigars when he grew up.

I remember very vividly it was the day after Christmas and everyone was having their siester in the afternoon. I had done the dishes, for once, and had grabbed a big fat cigar butt (dad's little treat) out of the ashtray. My brother was trying to blow a balloon up with the tyre pump when I beckoned to him to come out the front with me.

'Why!' he demanded in his usual bully boy fashion. I pretended not to notice and smiled at him.

'I've got something for you'. I said in a secretive voice, indicating that I had it in my pocket.

He looked delighted. Now before I go any farther you should know what sort of a little brother he was. He was a pain, always tattling on someone and getting them into trouble mostly for stuff he'd set 'em up to do. Then he'd stand back and laugh. If you were out anywhere he'd do his dandiest to show you up, you know, embarrass the heck out of you. Especially in front of boys and that is downright unforgivable.

Now that's cleared up back to the story. Bruce, my nearest and dearest little brother followed me out the front to see what I had for him. He was a tad suspicious and lagged behind a little.

Then we were out the front in the sleep out. I produced the cigar which was still a good three inches long and the box of matches. His eyes took on a gleam and his mouth hung open in a drooling smile which went quickly into a drooling grin.

He lifted his eyes to mine with a sort of hero worship. I almost, almost, felt sorry for him.

'Here' I said in a soft voice to hide the hysteria behind my kind and gentle demeanour. I poked the cigar in his gob; it was covered in drool in no time flat. 'Now suck' I said as I held the match to the cigar.

It was really so hard for him to suck with that grin on his face and it took him a few sucks to get her fired up. He squirmed a bit as the smoke found its way into his eyes and up his nose.

'Now' I said using my best informative air, 'do the draw back.'

'What?' he said the cigar nearly falling from his mouth, his bullyboy demeanour returning a tad, which was good or I might have felt sorry for him.

'Suck the smoke back into your lungs like this,' I took the cigar and demonstrated the draw back for the charmer with the grin.

'Oh I got it' he snapped and snatched the cigar back out of my hands.

I held my breath I really did, not thinking of the disaster this one stupid act could cause. Well I was twelve.

Bruce put the cigar to his mouth, took a real hard pull on it and sucked that smoke right back into his lungs. It shot right back out again like a bat out of hell; he doubled over his eyes bulged and shiny. His hands went to his neck and stayed there, his face turned red before it went purple; the silly grin was nowhere to be seen. Mind you I wasn't grinning either; he was making' enough noise to wake the dead and my family when they were asleep.

I swooped and grabbed up the cigar and put it out before I threw it out the window. Get rid of the evidence was my second nature not just my motto.

'Holy cow!' I said, 'make a bit more bloody noise why don't ya' Bruce was on his knees now and coughing himself inside out but at least he was able to get his breath a bit now after I hit him in the back a couple of times.

He looked up at me but he was unable to speak and I suspect he had a couple of things to say. I shot across the room and was listening at the door for sounds that we may have disturbed, I say, disturbed someone. Nothing. I breathed a sigh of relief as I went back to ask my brother the question.

I looked first at the mess he'd made on the floor, spit everywhere and pewk. Christ in heaven he was being' sick and one guess who'd have to clean it up. Now he was groaning and making a fuss, I had to ask him if he wanted mother to come in right at this minute and see what her darling little boy was up to.

'No' he shook his head. He was very clear on that.

'Thank god' I thought, he can speak at least now and he seems to have regained his senses.

I bent down to whisper in his ear, 'Bruce' I said softly . . .

'Shut your gob!' was his croaked reply.

'Thankyou' I said back in softly spoken tone. 'In a minute. But now tell me Bruce, do you still want to smoke cigars when you grow up?'

I never got an answer and well he's forty odd now and yes he's smoked a few cigars.

I myself and my good sister have given up the smokes but not without a fight. My brother I believe is still fighting the good fight. Love that man; glad he survived being my little brother.

## Chapter 13

# THE CHARGED DOG

By now anyone who has read some of my stories will realize that I grew up in the great Australian outback. The first years of my life were spent living in a tent as most people did up in that country. The roads weren't good enough for the most part to tow caravans in there in those days so one did the best they could. As time went by we did eventually move up to a caravan. Dad bought a brand new one in Broken Hill for one hundred pounds. That's given it away I think.

It was 1960 and the caravan was the old blister type and made from very light weight and very flimsy material. My mother was thrilled with it as she said she was up off the ground and the creepy crawlies which included such callers as snakes, scorpion's centipedes ECT. I can't say as I blame her.

I remember we were crossing the river at Blanch Town on the ferry must have been in '62 I reckon. We were on our way from the mallee in the south east of South Australia back up to Queensland as dad had been approached by a rabbit buyer named George Jesser to trap rabbits for him up there. The rabbits were lousy up there dad told mum at the tea table one night.

Anyhow to cut a long story short the old ford decided she'd boil and boil she did, all over the motor on the way up the bank on the other side. I was eight and was traveling in the caravan with my sister who was eleven, you could do that back then.

The ford gave up the ghost about half way up the bank, she over ran the hand brake and then the foot brake and the van rolled back and smashed into the safety chains which sided the ferry. When my mother pulled us out of the caravan it was hanging over the river, the wheels just inches from going over the side. Dozens of tourist and holiday makers flocked down to give a push and this rime she went all the way up and over the bank. 'Thank Christ for that' I heard dad say to mum later. The old ford had no rego'.

About six months later my dad got a bill for four pounds for the damage he caused to the ferry. I think the old man had it hung up on the wall for months. I don't think he paid it either but it made for a great talking piece.

Anyhow what was I on about, oh the outback dogs. We always kept a good cattle dog up there for protection. They could save your life in the event that a bull wished to make his way straight through the camp. I mean there was nothing to the caravan which would stop him now.

On the way back up there we called in at some outstation where we got a blue healer cross sissy. We didn't know that of course. But this old dog survived being run over twice by the trailer and another time a meal laced with 10-80 strychnine. It's what they used to bait dingoes with.

I shall never forget that day. Dad and Gordon had just got home from going round their traps. The dog dad had named boozer staggered into camp and slumped against a drum and slid to the ground where he stayed, breathing funny and foaming at the mouth.

'Bloody poison' dad yelled out to Gordon. Dad was on his feet in a flash and. he looked about wildly as he shouted to mum to bring him some salt 'the whole bloody packet' he roared.

He found what he was looking for hanging up in a tree, a length of hose. Into this he poured about half a packet of salt then handed it back to mum. He then forced one end of the hose down the dog's throat and put the other end in his mouth. He blew all the salt into the nearly unconscious dog which was too crook to do anything else but swallow.

We looked on in horror, able to do nothing, wanting to do something.

Dad picked poor old Boozer up by the hind legs and swung that dog around and around till he fell to the ground at which time Gordon picked him up and carried it on till he fell to the ground. This went on for a while and just as the two men had had it and fell to the ground too dizzy and exhausted to get to their feet the dog spewed violently all the poisoned meat that he'd eaten.

The three of them made quite a sight laying on the ground covered in dog pewk but the old dog lived to see another day. In fact we had him for years after that.

So this old dog's job was to chase way any bulls who threatened the camp see. Well it wasn't too long after the poison episode that he got his first opportunity.

It was a strange moonlit night you know when the sky is covered by thin white clouds and moon light sifts through and makes a real eerie light.

We were all brought bolt upright in our beds by a hell of a bellow about a couple hundred meters from the van. We all knew what it was, mum signaled for us to be quiet though she herself appeared to be on the verge of screaming herself. Dad was out round his traps and so that left just us, mum, me Judith and Bruce shaking in our beds in the darkness and the dog under the van.

We looked out the window and froze. He was a huge bloody thing standing in the moonlight, tossing his massive head and bellowing and pouring the ground. His horns must have been at least six feet from tip to tip.

We heard a thump as Boozer left the safety of the caravan to charge the bull and so get rid of the dangerous beast away from the camp. That was the plan, so far so good. And he sounded pretty good growling and barking as he went.

But as the dog got closer to the bull he started to slow up, the bull put his head down and charged him. Boozer, of course, turned and ran back to the safety of the caravan and the bull was right behind him.

'Oh Holy mother of god . . . .' My mum started to pray. The bull was almost upon us and we all thought he was coming right through.

We all screamed at once I was too scared to much more than yell 'no, no, no'. And the bull slowed to a stop just a few meters from the van obviously taken aback by our ear splitting screams. Did you like that huh, 'taken aback'? A bloody wild bull taken aback. Phh! But he stopped.

We fell silent and our legs gave out from under us as he threw his head back and bellowed again, I mean he bloody roared. There isn't another sound more blood curdling in this country. We sat petrified as the dog thumped and rattled under the van trying, no doubt, to find the safest part.

Now the bull inched closer and closer till his breath started fogging up the window that I was too paralysed to leave. Again and again he breathed in my face, nothing but a bit of glass between us. I sat motionless, hardly game enough to breath. He was listening and then he started sniffing, I could hear him and I remembered being told that animals could smell your fear. No problems here I would have reeked.

He tried to step around for a better look I suppose, and tripped over the A frame tow bar which was just sitting on a four gallon drum. The caravan lurched, he panicked and ran off and the A frame dropped in the dirt with a jolt and we yelled blue murder once again.

Then silence total silence. We were all exhausted and we sat where we were, too scared stiff to move anyway and that's; how dad found us. Didn't he laugh when we told him how the great Aussie cattle dog brought the bull back to the caravan with him. Not supposed to happen. Still who could blame him and he did try didn't he?

Well we found he was more of a sheep dog really and went on looking for a dog who could do the job and that was how we ended up with a dog, a very good cattle dog, who we named Skipper. But that's another story.

So thanks again for letting me get that off my chest, you know I still have nightmares about bulls. I love going to rodeos though, must've got something twisted somewhere along the line. You won't find me getting in with em though.

Cheers mate see you in the long paddock one day huh.

# Chapter 14

# THE BLITZ AND THE WEAPON CARRIER

Mum stood with her hands to her face, she was agitated, tears wet on her flushed cheeks, 'Oh my beautiful caravan! How bad is it Arthur?' she cried 'Can you fix it? Will it be all right?'

'Just give me two minutes to have a look' Dad sounded tired and exasperated, the strain evident on his face. Roy came up and took a look and then looked up at my mother pacing up and

'Don't look to good hay Art.' He kept his voice down low so that mum wouldn't hear him.

Dad stopped and looked at mum, 'well I can fix it' he said 'but we'll need to call in at Milawertana Station. The chassis is gonna need welding and I don't have the equipment.' He looked at the people who were now standing around then back at mum. 'And the back end of it's been almost completely dragged out of it but I can fix that to, the kids won't be able to sleep down there till I do so we'll have to fix em up on the floor.'

'Well if that's what we gotta do then that's what we'll do Art' Teddy said to dad. He'd just walked up and stood there trying to light his pipe and keep his beard from going up at the same time. He didn't always succeed by the way. I remember one day he was sitting in the caravan with mum and dad having a cuppa. Well he got his pipe out and after he'd lit it up he was swinging the match from side to side over his shoulder to put it out and up went mums lovely lace curtains. I thought mum was going to try to throw him out through the window.

Dad turned to him now, 'I'm gonna have to stop here till I get that van ready to tow again so if you blokes want to go on I'll understand. We'll catch up somewhere along the track.'

'No, we're gunna wait' says Teddy 'we all stay together right? Like always Art.'

Dad smiled at him and went back to working. We had just come through the Flinders Rangers and one of the creeks was a bit steep and the chassis had gotten twisted in the process and now it was almost broken right through.

We were travelling north as we'd had good reports that the rabbits were thick up there. I mean a lot of them; I am not casting aspersions on their intellect. Back then rabbits were big business.

We had quite a convoy to, Roy and Fred and Fay were travelling with us in a big old dodge Ute. Bob came to with his old blitz; Teddy was next with his weapon carrier and his old dog that didn't like anyone, And the McLean's family with their truck and four tents six kids and a big old playful dog that just seemed to get in the way all the time.

There was the Woodford's, a large family of eight and the Bruges another large family then there was Rowdy and Nell and all their progeny, which numbered about four I think.

Young Brian travelled with us also and had brought with him a couple of mates whose names I can't remember. They had an FJ Holden which was pretty flash going in those days. Damn thing was always breaking down though. Sorry Holden lovers I think he just bought a lemon you know. God knows I've had enough of those to qualify me as an expert.

We were headed right up to Queensland and we were all hanging out to reach the border and the dog fence. We always loved to get to Queensland for some reason or other. I still love Queensland.

We'd had a delay at Cleve and we'd all had to make camp for a few days to make some running repairs and the stopover had worked out fairly costly. We made camp outside of Cleve just off the road in a secluded little area and settled in for the duration. None of the vehicles were registered and so my dad told everyone to stay in camp and don't go out and get caught 'if one goes we'll all go' he told them. 'We'll sneak through the towns late at night.' That was the plan. And it had always worked in the past.

Well anyway, young fellas being' as young fella's are, Brian and the boys went off to town to get a drink or two. To cut a long story short they did attract the attention of the local constabulary and being boys they decided to outrun the coppers and get back to camp before they got into any more strife.

Well they got back to camp all right and the 'coppers' had a field day booking everyone for things from unregistered to no licence to bald tyres and no brakes. Everyone got done! I think we paid for the new damn they'd just put in at Rudall.

So the trip had not been without its ups and downs and since leaving the Nullarbor we had been on the road for three weeks already. The weather was getting worse and we wanted to be up in Queensland before it turned wet.

We camped that night on the creek bank where we had done the damage to the caravan. The thing I remember most about that particular trip was mums old trestle table. Every tea time this old table was unfolded and a tablecloth put over it and it was set properly. Out came the four gallon drums we used for chairs and we'd sit at this table set fit for a king. Rabbit stew if we were lucky but our table was very grand and our manners had to be impeccable. Even if bread and dripping was on the menu for tonight we sat at table. And we were clean!

We crossed the Flinders Ranges just north of Quorn and that had its troubles to. The car my mum was driving had no brakes and so the plan was for mum to travel close up behind Rowdies car and if it became necessary he would pull us up. Wow! I have never been so scared. But we made it and nobody's car got even damaged. All that day I tried to keep my head buried under a rug but to no avail. I just had to look.

We stayed two days at the station and got the caravan fixed up. The weather was fair and so my sister and I slept out on the ground. We loved it anyway sleeping under the stars. I still to this day prefer to sleep with the windows and curtains opened.

From there we cut through the corner country and headed into Queensland. It had started to rain and bogging was a constant problem. It slowed us down and what should have been a few days trip turned into weeks on the road. We were all tired to the point of exhaustion and hungry to the point of starvation. No kidding.

We wouldn't have done it at all except for the old weapon carrier. What a machine that was. To look at it was like these utes they have now and put giant wheels on them. The old blitz did a magnificent job to and I take my hat off the engineering. Six-wheel drive it was and nothing stopped it. Not even Big Ben at its worst. Big Ben was a particularly nasty sand hill which sometimes became just impassable and so you had to go round it. You could never go over it in a two wheel drive.

Back to the story; it all takes time to bog one vehicle and then you have to hook it up to the weapon carrier or the blitz, and then you have to unhook when you finally get free of the bog. It all takes time and can delay a trip of say two days to weeks.

The worst time was while we were travelling along the dingo proof fence and it had been raining for a couple of days. We got the land rover with the caravan on behind bogged to the chassis and so we hooked it up to the old weapon carrier and dad sang out to Teddy to take her away. Old Teddy waves and gives it the gas and down she went, bloody great tractor tyres an all. Bogged to the axle.

In unison, everyone there turned to look at the old blitz. She looked smaller than she ever had done before and a bit ramshackle but she was all we had. Our only ace left to play.

The thing to consider here was the fact that we were very short on supplies with everyone on ration already. Now if we hooked the blitz up to the weapon carrier and bogged that to then no one was going anywhere. And perishing out in these places in these times was not unheard of. Finally Bob decided that he thought she could do it and what the hell . . .

Old Bob climbed up into the front seat, me beside him, and he backed her up to the weapon carrier. Dad and Teddy found a length of rope and hooked her up to the other vehicles. The plan was that if the blitz started to go under then we'd stop and unhook the rover and caravan.

Bob fired up the old blitz, Teddy fired up the old weapon carrier and dad fired up the old land rover. And for some reason I jumped down out of the blitz to watch, I just wanted to watch. And what a sight it was!

Slowly and laboriously the old diesel motors of the blitz and weapon carrier gathered momentum, thundering and shuddering the two motors joined by the grunt of the land rover rose to a crescendo.

The air was thick with diesel fumes and petrol smoke, the motors all screaming. And just as slowly and just as laboriously the old weapon carrier came up out of its bog followed by the rover and van. We were free. And we were saved. No one perishing on this day.

The rest of the trip went fairly uneventful and we made it to the greener pastures of Queensland and for a time prospered reasonably well. Every inch of every journey out there was a struggle and an adventure but somehow arriving was more special.

And I take my hat off to the fighting spirit of these old diggers home from the war, and their families who suffered hardship after tyring hardship to open up this big country. Before the oil drillers and the government surveyors the mining companies before all these. The diggers with nowhere else they can go, a country trying to forget all about em and the bloody war nothing to their names but what they carried. And when the old diggers retreated one last time into the great out back of Australia it was without the gratitude of those who made them what they were. But they took with them the ultimate in rewards, given them by their fellow countrymen, a thing more important to them than any other thing. Their freedom.

They are all dead now God rest em all those men who made up my circle of friends, my social calendar as it were. I never heard one of em complain about what he had or didn't have or what had happened to em. They were given their freedom and for that ultimate reward, the digger, well he'd paid the ultimate price. His peace of mind.

When that trip ended we got ourselves a couple of dingos and they were among the best friends I ever had and I'm sure my sister will agree. And unlike most of the human friends I made along the way, when a dingo becomes your friend you become pack and there is nothing they won't do for you or share with you. And it breaks my heart that we can't find it in us to share this beautiful land with these most beautiful of God's creatures.

The fine and noble dingo, a fitting mate for a fine and noble digger don't you think?

Anyhow that's another story and thanks again for letting me get it off my chest. As usual I have enjoyed the telling and the memories.

I say a prayer every night of my life for the old diggers, alive or dead and for the dingo also alive or dead. And I thank god for the time I had with them and the lessons I learned from them

# Chapter 15

# WITH DINGOES I SLEPT TILL MORNING

I might have mentioned in earlier stories, the fact that we had a couple of dingoes when we were up in Queensland. I should probably say they had us for they relied on us for nothing. Whenever they went hunting they brought something back for me, usually rabbits. I followed them one day it was a beautiful day just after the rain and everything was fresh.

The air was fresh and cool and fluffy white clouds raced across the sky. I used to like to run and stay in their shadow. On such days I would get to dreaming about all sorts of stuff and how I wanted to write a story one day.

This day was no exception and I passed through from the land I knew to the land I didn't without notice. And when it came time to go home and I realized I was lost I felt the cold hand of terror in my belly once again and it hurts! I called out to my dingo friends but they were on the trail of something and ran off and left me. I looked around at the landscape trying to find my direction but none came to me. Nothing familiar stood out. I put my hands to my chest, I was five and not yet at school. And I knew what these cold desert nights were like. The temperature got down so low the water in the taps froze solid.

I sat down and put my head on my knees and began to cry. Softly at first and then louder and louder until I was bawling my head off. I was silent again and sat listening to the sounds of the bush. It was late afternoon and the nocturnal animals would be rising soon. The predatory dingo would take over from the eagles and snakes. And my mum would be cooking dinner.

I wished for my mum and even dad and I even promised I would be a good girl hence forth and for the whole rest of my life. I started to shiver. No matter how I rubbed my chest the pain wouldn't go away. I couldn't just sit there so I got up and did the worst thing I could have done. I walked round in circles.

All too soon it was getting dark and I still had no clue where I was. I didn't know what to do. If I sat down I got cold, I didn't even have on a jumper. Just a cotton dress. I flopped in the dirt once more and I remembered that song about the little boy lost. How it had always made me sad. I hoped for a happy ending to my tale too.

I heard a snuffling sound behind me and a joyous grin spread over my face as I swung round to greet my dingoes. 'Shit!' that was all I could think of. These were not my dingoes. The one doing the snuffling was a beautiful big animal and showed no fear as he got closer to me.

I stood still, nothing much else I could do. Finally he was just about twenty paces from me. He looked up at me and snarled. The most blood curdling snarl I can remember and I have been snarled at by all manner of dogs. I talked to him, it made no difference. I turned my face away and he stopped growling. But now I could see his pack. Holy shit I said to myself there's a whole pack of 'em. Must have been about ten. My legs were going quite weak but I stayed on my feet.

So far in life's travels nothing had prepared me for this. Suddenly one of the dingoes from the pack to the right of me lunged at me. She knocked me flying and I hit the dirt with a thud and a sob. I did not scream and I have not screamed to this day. I think those dingoes frightened it out of me. I can yell yes but scream no.

I sat sobbing in the dirt and was dimly aware that it was getting dark, I was also aware that more dingoes were arriving on the scene. I couldn't look. My eyes took in only the red dirt and the green of the spinifex bush I had landed near. What could I do, I was buggered and I knew it. 'Mum' I sobbed into the gathering dusk 'oh please mum come and get me.' My hands came up and covered my face 'where are you dad?' The only thing that was going to save me now was a miracle. My dad always said that a dingo will only attack a man if it's very hungry. That wasn't much comfort.

Another snarl, this one in my ear brought my head down lower. A few more snarls and I couldn't help but notice the dingoes had backed off a bit, or had they? A dingo came up close to me and I flicked my eyes up to see what was happening and couldn't believe my eyes,

My two darling dingoes stepped forward and stood in front of me. One of, Them, Sheg, sat down and they did some yipping noises, a bit more snarling and the leader of the pack stood up and turned to leave. But the bitch to my right had something to say which made the lead dog turn and snarl at her. She walked passed me and nuzzled one of my dingoes, the one who was sitting. He jumped to his feet and made for me and as he got behind me I found my stride.

I jumped to my feet and started yelling at these dogs and waving my hands about. The bitch, whom I suspected had taken a fancy to Sheg, the smallest of my dingoes. Came towards me. I knew enough about nature and animals to know that a dog won't hurt a bitch and I was in trouble me and my big mouth.

Surprising me, Sheg stood up and barred her way while Bosun kept watch on the leader. Everything went quiet for a few moments and then the leader dog turned to go and I heaved a sigh of relief. I knew better than to make eye contact with them at this stage of proceedings.

It was this leader dog who finally called the shots. He gave an almighty growl and the dingoes including the trouble making bitch followed him away. Sheg darted over to a bush and loped back with a half-eaten rabbit for me. I was too weak and exhausted to do anymore and I flopped in the dirt I smiled at his huge lolloping grin and passed out.

I came to and it was dark and cold. I was so cold it was really painful and felt a little like my skin was burning. I sobbed and immediately heard a snuffle and a warm body lay down beside me. 'Bosun' I sobbed as I put my arm around him and cried for my mum and dad and my sister. Another warm body lay in the dirt on the other side of me and I felt really quite snug and safe. And thus with the dingoes I slept till morning.

I awoke with a start and looked around me. My dilemma returned to me in waves of terror but at least it was daylight. Just. The dingoes were running around playing, how I envied them their lack of fear. Me, well I was already hungry and thirsty. Not hungry enough to have a go at the half eaten rabbit though. I looked about for it and found it where Sheg had dropped it. I picked it up and took it over to them, but they took no notice.

I yelled at them to be quiet and listen, and they did. Both sat upright looking at me Bosun's tongue lolling from the side of his mouth. He looked so comical I laughed. I laughed and laughed till my sides ached.

Bosun ran to me and knocked me sideways into the dirt. I couldn't stop laughing. Sheg ran in and grabbed a mouthful of my dress and growled deep in his throat as I tried to get my breath enough to tell him to let go. I was so weak from terror and laughing and hunger that I just let him pull me around in the dirt like a sack giving me a good shake now and then. Bosun ran in also growling that playful growl deep in his throat and grabbed my shoe and began pulling me the other way. I still could not stop laughing.

When the shot rang out it took a while to register what had happened, even when Sheg collapsed in my lap. I screamed 'don't, don't, don't.' as I threw myself across him. There was absolute silence.

I got to my feet and faced the man with the gun and yelled at him if he shot another bullet I would bite his fingers off. I looked down at Sheg who was breathing heavily in the dirt. Tears welled in my eyes and I couldn't see a thing. I felt myself being lifted up into strong arms and

I heard dad tell the man not to shoot, 'those are her dingoes' he said. 'Gordon, get the damn thing up out of the dirt and put him in the back. You to' he said to bosun but Bosun ran home.

I didn't see him do it I still couldn't see. Even when I stopped crying I still couldn't see and I could not speak. My threat at the man with the gun was the last thing I said for many long weeks though slowly my sight returned to me. I wanted to tell mum all about it but they reckon the fear had been too much and put me in shock or some damn thing like that. All I know is that something broke inside me when I saw Sheg fall down dead or so I thought. Something that took time to heal.

Then when Sheg got up from his bed one day and took off, with a funny limp after Bosun to play I let out a howl. No one could believe it. I howled the howl of a dingo and Bosun and Sheg stopped what they were doing to listen. They put their heads back and howled back and ran off to go hunting. I wriggled to get free from my dad's grip but he said 'oh no Mary girl, not today.'

Mum and dad told me later that the men had been out looking for me and when they saw the dingoes pulling me around in the dirt he thought they were ripping me to pieces. I thought about it and knew beyond a doubt that the man did what he thought was best. He thought he was saving my life. He had shot Sheg in the ribs but the bullet had passed through without doing any major damage.

When I said goodbye to those dingoes a year or so later I thought I'd never get over it. And I was right. But they were always wild dogs, they had just formed an alliance with a timid little girl and they let me share their precious time. I had been part of their pack and they had proved themselves to be among the best friends I ever had.

I still wonder what exactly took place out there in the middle of nowhere amongst the red sand hills with the spinifex and daises. Small puddles of water here and there with mapou bushes and mulga trees haphazardly around the landscape. Perfect! A truly beautiful land if you aint lost in it. Maybe somebody out there can help me put together what happened. Maybe I'm not supposed to know.

Anyhow that's life aint it I thank my lucky stars they were there when I needed them. And thank you for listening to me huh. Till next time then

The end

# Chapter 16
## NINE LIVES OR TEN

This is a story about a cat, a very different kind of cat that I had years ago as a kid. I have been inspired to tell this story by an old cat I met up at the Copley caravan and Cabin Park a little while ago. Copley is a little town up near Leigh Creek. It is really uncanny because this old cat is black with a diamond shaped patch of white on its throat.

I said to the lady who belonged to the cat that I had once belonged to a cat exactly like that and I'd gotten him not far from here years ago. 'His name was Middy' I said. 'Short for Midnight diamond. What's his name?' I asked politely indicating the bone idle cat slouching in the warm sunshine at her feet.

She looked at me for a moment, somewhat aghast, and then she replied 'his name is Midnight Diamond' she smiled.

'Unreal,' I said, 'how did the old bloke lose his paw?' I asked.

She told me she didn't know he just kind of showed up one day and it was gone. 'The wound had kept him home for a few days' she told me as she bent down to stroke his chin.

I told her that the old cat I had I'd gotten on an out station on Worterloona not far from Copley about thirty years ago. My sister and I had gone there with my dad. to see the man who lived there about something or other I'm not sure what.

My sister and I got bored with the conversation and so decided to go exploring.

It was early on in this exploration that we came across the kittens, a whole box of em. We couldn't believe our luck. Six kittens, all different colours. My sister selected a nice grey one and I myself chose a lovely black one with a white throat as I have mentioned.

But then there was this little brown one we just couldn't go without so we picked him up to and off we went to convince dad that we needed them all.

Well we must have done an excellent job because when we got in the land rover to go home we had the kittens in a box on the floor in the back with us.

My sister and I used to stand up in the back of the four wheel drive and lean our elbows on the cabin, we went everywhere like that and we were riding thus when we were nearing home on that day. An argument had started up between us as arguments do, about who would be telling mum about the cats. Well at this stage we were still under the impression that mum would be pleased about it. The argument heated up and got louder and fiercer with a good measure of threats and name calling thrown in.

Of course, in his defence, my father would have been sick of listening to this bickering from the back by now. We got into it, Jude and me for sure.

You might remember that back then the clothes line was a piece of wire strung from one tree to another with a pole in the middle to hold it up high. So in the middle of our bickering we hadn't noticed that he'd swung round to take us under the thing. So the bloody clothes line caught us fair under the chin, marched us backwards, the tail gate got us right in the back of the knees, over we went and the rest as they say is history. I do remember also that I was the first up out of the dirt and so I was first in to tell mum the good news, again under the impression that she'd be thrilled.

Except that it didn't look much like good news on Mum's face as she marched outside to see dad shoving me out of the way as she went. I was crushed. I should not, after what he had done, feel one iota of sympathy for my father but I did. Especially after the fight he put up so that we could keep the kittens.

Any way that is how I came by the cat by the name of Midnight Diamond who went by the name of Middy. Nothing to do with beer. Well this cat was huge with a broad head and massive shoulders. I have seen that car fight cattle dogs and send them running. None of the men would touch him.

We had a dog called patch who was all heart and no brain. He wandered under the house one day, which was on stilts as they often are in Queensland, for his afternoon siesta. Well see, the cat was under there and didn't' feel much like company and that old dog came out from under that house like a bat out of hell. Making a noise also like something from hell and the old cat was running along after him up on his hind legs swinging at the dogs butt so's even I felt sorry for him. Patch scaled a five foot fence to safety but then I had to open the gate for him to come back in. I guess the incentive wasn't there anymore, the motivation to jump it. And whenever Dad killed a sheep or something, the cat ate first.

He'd go hunting of a night time and I'd wake up with a half-eaten duck and one time a half-eaten field rat on my chest, the back end, I always got the back end. And they were nearly always wet.

One day in the middle of summer we had a down pour. A monsoonal storm of such magnitude that the water banked up for a mile or so from the catchments tank for the dam. They're called settling pools in some places. Anyway the water poured into the catchments and ran through about twenty feet of pipe and then into the dam. So on the one side there was a whirl pool and then the water roared out the other side into the dam.

Kids being as kids are we wanted to go and watch such a spectacle, but we kept a respectable distance from it the ground was all slippery clay. Well to cut a long story short the dog was not using his brain this day and when he spotted the whirlpool he had to have a good look. His heart obviously told him so. Before you could bat an eye lid we heard a splash and turned to stare. He'd jumped in and was off to do just that.

We screamed franticly as we watched that tired old dog get closer to the whirlpool.

Middy stopped what he was doing and stood stock still and watched. The bird he'd been stalking flew noisily into the sky. I still remember that cat's eyes, wide with disbelief. No scorn, no anger just disbelief.

Back in the water the old dog realized his mistake and tried to turn away from the whirlpool but he couldn't. He struggled there for ages but he was just getting too weary. He splashed around frantically for what seemed to be an eternity.

He wasn't even holding his ground now and was being pulled closer to the whirlpool. It was obvious he was in a panic the poor old beggar was panting so hard we could hear him above the roar of the water and the screeching birds.

Everything seemed suddenly to stand still, all eyes on the massive fight the old dog was putting up. My sister went to head off and get dad but we knew there was no time. We watched in trepidation the chilling scene in the swirling muddy water.

Next thing we saw a black streak in the air up behind Patch. Middy had launched himself from the top of the pipe and landed just behind the old dog. Chaos! Middy whacked that dog's backside until the dog got his second wind. The dog found a new strength only cats claws could induce.

Middy, like most cats, hated to get wet and he appeared to be very annoyed. The dog swam for his life and the cat turned to follow him.

Only now see the cat had gotten caught up in the swirling water of the whirlpool himself. The old dog made it to the bank where he shook himself until those around him were good and wet.

I stood on the bank and watched my dear old cat battle the muddy water with all his might. Then I watched him disappear from sight. We, my sister and brother and the old dog and me, stood in silence.

A movement out of the corner of my eye brought my head up, the others followed my gaze. A dripping wet, huge black cat came over the bank; shaking his feet as he came. He'd been spat out the other side and he was mad and worse he was indignant.

'Hooray' we all cried, and things like 'thank god', 'thank goodness' and 'good old Middy.'

However we all had the good sense not to go near him. All that is instead of Patch, who in his gratitude, let his heart take him right to within striking distance of a very wet very miserable and oh so ornery cat. He did the unthinkable and licked Middy's face.

Middy just looked at him for a while and turned away to walk home with all the dignity he could muster. And we all let out our breath as we watched him walk off.

I then, so moved by all this, ran up and picked him up so grateful to have him come back and got the worst flogging I've ever had from an animal in my entire life and that's as true as god is. And when I finally got his claws unhooked from my face I threw him back in the water. A couple of days later there was the customary half of his kill when

I woke up in the morning. A dead duck which had been plucked in my bedroom, his half missing, mine on my chest. All was forgiven it seemed.

Well it's been therapy alright, till the next monsoon then. Cheers.

# Chapter 17

# RIP VAN WINKLE

This is a story about one of the most colourful characters I've ever met and God knows I've met em all. This old guy could have been anywhere between sixty and a hundred, you had no way of knowing. Even he didn't recall how old he was.

He'd attended both world wars and I think Korea. He was a tall man must have been six feet at least. He had wide shoulders which were still surprisingly straight. These old diggers were all the same with the straight backs and all. I wouldn't mind betting that's how they know each other to be vets you know, the straight backs. When I was a kid my father was always instructing us in how we should hold ourselves for good posture. He had us walking like bloody soldiers by the time we were seven or eight years old.

Any way the first time I'd ever encountered this old man was one day when we called in to see some friends who lived on an outstation in the northern most Flinders Rangers. We hadn't seen them for a couple of years so mum and dad decided to surprise them. However they were gone the old bloke who was living there now informed us. 'Left here about six months back' he says 'anyway come in for a cupper, mate have yiz eaten?'

'No' dad says 'Thanks mate a cupper'd go down real good hay. If you're sure it's no trouble.'

'No trouble mate, no trouble at all' he says as he shook dad's hand.

We jumped down out of the back of the four wheel drive, always excited to meet new people especially old ancients like this guy. I could feel some wonderful stories coming on.

'You'll stay for tea mate wont ya? Ya welcome to stay the night to.' He'd shaken hands with dad and held his hand out to mum as she came round the car to meet him.

I'm up the front there waiting for dad to introduce me, I mean this guy looked like Rip Van Winkle himself. He had lines criss crossing lines and a long white beard. And he'd asked us to stay the night, and have tea. I looked at dad anxiously but he didn't answer. But what he did was, he introduced mum and told me to go and play. Play!

I gave him my best glare and I hoped that my bitter disappointment was clear. But no, he gives me a crooked sort of a grin and turned around and strode onto the house. My mouth was hanging opened when I heard a chuckle from my sister.

'What's so bloody funny?' I asked spreading my hands in exasperation. 'We've been told to go and play.'

She didn't answer she was staring after them, 'wonder how old he is' she says as the back door bangs shut on us.

Well I was flabbergasted mate, I was. Just then the door opens up again and the old guy sticks his head out 'come on kids' he says 'come and have a cupper n some biscuits.'

No need to ask me twice, so I puts on me best smile and marched, straight backed, just like I been taught, fair into the old guys kitchen.

Oh and what a kitchen it was, straight out of some sort of pirate movie. Shit, I thought, the old guys a pirate had to be. He had a sword hangin on the wall and over on the cupboard he had a ship in a bottle. No joke, a ship in a bottle.

I looked at Jude but she was unimpressed so I looked at dad. He was laughing at something the old guy had said. I stood at the table now looking straight at my old man waiting for an intro but none was forth coming. Dad's manners could be atrocious at times, that's all I could think of.

I sat at the table and accepted my cup of tea and biscuits with good grace. I kept my eyes fixed on Rip now and waited for the stories to start, and I was not disappointed; we listened well into the night.

He'd been everywhere, fought everything even dad was impressed I could see that. I looked at my sister with disdain; she was asleep on mums shoulder. Sometimes the old man got a bit excited and made a funny hooting noise in his throat but that only added to the flavour. Or so I thought.

Dad stopped listening at around midnight and I wondered at how quiet he'd been for the last half hour or so. He looked troubled like he was waiting for something. Something bad. I shrugged it off, shit these stories were funny and so exciting!

A bit after midnight the old guy goes quiet and stares at the door to the back of the house. Dad gets up quietly and in an equally quiet voice he says to the old guy that we had to hit the hay. 'Go on kids, get out to the caravan.'

I looked up at him for some sort of explanation and got a shove.

All of a sudden the old guy lets out a yell that just about rooted me to the spot. Well it did! 'The bastards are back' he sings out and darted into the dark adjoining room which had a bit of torn cloth of no apparent colour hanging from the top of the door frame.

He returns with, of all things, an old pump action, double barrel straight out of the cowboy era. And this old gun was all loaded up, cocked and ready to make some noise.

Now, see we're all standing rooted to the spot and dads trying to get mum to move but she don't want to go passed the now maniac with the gun. And he was waving that bloody thing around as he went. Anyhow Rip throws the thing on the table and rips his shirt off and threw that to the floor.

'Get your bloody clothes off' he says and dad started. He looked down at the gun on the other side of the table The old guys screaming by this about dingoes and how they'd been stalking him for the last few months but he had always sent them running. Well that explains the holes in the doors I swung round to look, buckshot!

And right there in front of my eyes he let her rip, both barrels, took out the light the glass window, the fly screen my hearing and dad's sense of humour. Next I got dad's hand in the middle of my back and was hurled none too gently to the floor. Then Jude and mum landed where he threw them. I had questions I wanted to ask but I figured this wasn't a good time.

Dad was off, he cleared the table, two bounds and he had the old fulla by the neck, I knew this because I could see their silhouettes in the doorway.

What I couldn't see was where the next shot, fired from a lesser gun, probably a hand gun I thought, ended up.

Mum was screaming 'Arthur, Arthur.' while I lay there on the floor snivelling into my sleeve.

'I'm alright mother shut up and quieten the kids down.' Dad was still wrestling with Genghis. The old guy was still raving about those sneaky, cunning, conniving dingoes so I guessed he was alright to. Dad wouldn't be going away to jail this time I hoped.

'Maida can you get that light going please so I can see.'

Mum finally, with shaky hands, got the light back on and we all looked at one another. The old geezer Looked at us and went quiet. He looked at us one by one as if he was seeing us for the first time. Dad lets him go! I didn't think that was one of his best ideas.

'I'm sorry' the old guy looks a bit perplexed, 'can I offer you a cupper mate?' He asks dad.

Dad clears his throat, 'we're sorry to call on you so late', he says 'but we must get going. We'll call in on the way back'.

Thank god that's over I thought as I let my shoulders sag. I wasn't sure what 'that' was but thank god it was over.

'Well you and your family must stay here the night and go on in the morning after a nice breakfast.' Shit this old guy was good. I don't for the life of me know how I knew he was faking. But faking he was.

'Well,' dad cleared his throat again; he was beginning to annoy me. 'We could sleep in the van and say good bye to morrow I suppose.' He looks at mum, she glares back not keen.

'Alright' the old guy's croonin now, 'a nice breaky before you go. What do you say?' He turns to mum now.

'Well, well . . .' Mum was no good at this stuff.

'Come on kids' dad says as he hauls Jude up off the floor against her will I think. She wasn't taken in either. 'Well not me, I don't want his bloody . . .' She got no farther and she got a shove towards the door. I stood and watched dad unload the gun, and he stuck the hand gun in his pocket and the old relic he puts back on the table. We were all skirting the room making for the back door.

'Are you going to be alright now?' dad asked Rip. The old guy nods dad looks him right in the eye 'Do I have your word on that Mac? No more guns?' The old guy nods again and his eye, his left eye only flicked, down at the gun on the table. A shiver passed through me.

Dad walked over to the old man and very gently and in reverence to the old soldiers past, he puts his hand out and shook hands with old Rip. Actually I think his name was Samuel. Samuel grinned up at dad his one and only tooths showing the results of yeas of smoking and drinking rum straight from the bottle.

'Rum!' the old boy yells as if he could read my thoughts. 'Ya wanna drink o' rum? I got a bottle o' the best damn rum you ever tasted son.'

Well I can't believe it, dad actually gave it some thought and without casting a glance at mum he says, 'no thanks mate. We'll be seein ya mate.'

We'd gotten out the back door across the yard and mum was on the top step of the caravan when we heard yet another shot from yet another gun. Jude and I, old hands at this by now believe it or not, hit the dirt once more.

I heard dad cursing as he turned and, crouching low, he ran back toward the house. We watched him go in the bright moonlight. Before he got half way across the yard, the moonlight almost as bright as day, we see the maniac come pelting out of the house his sawn off at the ready. Well first he blasted the somewhat grey sheets on the clothes line, accusing them as he did so of being in cohorts with those lousy stinking dingoes.

'Oh what is it with him and the dingoes.' My sister said not only out loud but very loud.

I looked at her, 'have you gone loco' I asked in a whisper? 'Shut the hell up.' She shrugged her shoulders as she sat up.

'Get down' I hissed at her.

'No' she shakes her head 'I'm sick of this.'

I looked aghast at her my mouth hanging open. I turned back to where dad was edging toward the old guy making no noise as he went.

The next blast took out the outhouse door and anything inside made out of porcelain. Oh well! In the moonlight we could see him reloading, my, he was fast. He thumbs the two new shells in and snaps the gun back into play seemingly in one motion. She's all ready to fire. Dad was just a few steps away when the old guy turns the gun on him.

'Hells bells' I heard him mutter as he hit the ground and rolled the rest of the way. Rip aims the gun at the ground too late as dad hits him in the shins and knocks him the hell over. As he goes down the gun goes off one more time and both the men lay still. In the quiet, eerie light of the moon I wondered if we were orphans or not.

It seemed like everything stayed quiet for ages but must have been only seconds. The moonlight was almost as bright as day I thought as I lifted my head higher for a better look. We lay still and held our breaths, muscles screaming unheard, as we waited to see how this had played out.

Just then we heard a creaking sound to our left and swung around to see the big old gum tree at the back of the house come down slowly towards the two forms lying on the ground.

Dad was on his feet and we breathed again but he was still in the path of the tree. He bent down and grabbed the old guy by the ankles and pulled him clear. Slowly and gently he pulled the old guy up onto his feet and held him steady for a few moments till he got his balance, or as my mum used to say 'he got his sea legs under him.' The old gum tree hit the dirt without another sound.

'Well it looks like I scored meself a couple of nice guns' dad says picking up the double barrel shotgun at his feet a wry smile on his face. He had the pistol in his pocket. 'Let's go' he says and we were in the Toyota in no time flat.

Well we decided not to stay any longer in that place and hit the road that night. The old guy, they told us at the next hut, was a bit looney but he was more of a danger to himself. Dunno if dad agreed with that or not.

'Thank Christ you took that bloody shotgun off him, none of us were game to go and see how he is.' The station manager said as he shook dad's hand 'No, you take the bloody gun mate and welcome. I dunno how many bloody guns he's got out there exactly but he's got a few less now and that can only be a good thing.'

What I thought was a hand gun of some description in the dark, turned out to be another sawn off! The station manager shook his head and handed it to dad. 'He's not a bad old man but . . .'

'I know mate' replied dad, 'He's been alone too long I think.'

Some years later dad and Jude and I went passed there again and yes he was still there. And that is where I got my cat called Midnight from whom I wrote you about in a tale I called 'Nine Lives or Ten'

Samuel was much better and didn't seem to recollect us as we were all introduced again. I have never forgotten him however and I'm probably not likely to anytime soon. And I don't think his forgetfulness was faked either on this last occasion but still, we didn't stay long this visit.

He'd be dead now of course so I would like to just say 'RIP' Samuel you will always be a hero to me. A mad one but still a hero.

Thanks for the memories and one of the most interesting evenings of my entire life. And of course, as usual I salute you Samuel, 'lest we forget'. Another hero, home from the war.

Until we meet again when I will tell you another tale from the sand hills it's goodbye and good luck.

# Chapter 18

# THE SKIPPER

Well I've mentioned the Skipper before and now I would love to tell you about a really great dog with a really great heart. We got him from a cattle station just north of the Queensland-NSW. Border fence and so he was a very well-bred dog if you wanted a cattle dog. He was a blue heeler.

I can remember when he was a puppy, we'd had him about a week, and some inquisitive emus came by. They crept up very slowly to get a good look at the caravan as emus do. Inside the caravan we all stayed quiet so's they'd come right up.

Next thing we hear this little growl and a tiny, fat little blue grey bundle came running (waddling) out from under the caravan, charged straight at em, and barked at those huge birds. And they turned and ran. You had to fall in love with the little bloke right there.

And so the love affair with our newest member began and there was never anything too much for that dog to take on when we needed him.

And, of course, sometimes when we didn't. I suppose I should mention the ego this dog had. But I won't. You can be the judge of that.

There was nothing this dog loved more than a good fight, except of course to win a good fight. If he ever got beaten he'd sweat off on the other dog and he'd start training so as to get ready. He'd run and jump and pick fights with lesser dogs and then when he was ready he'd go back and try again and he'd do this until he won.

I know nowadays this sort of thing may be frowned upon but he lived in hard times and he was a hard dog. When he got hurt he expected no sympathy, praise yes but sympathy no.

This dog would get a set on people to, anyone my father didn't like. It seemed like dad was forever apologizing and wiping up the blood of those that he himself, didn't like. Old Skipper was very protective of his whole family I recall.

We were messing around out at the fire one night my sister and I playing some silly game with this old workmate of dads. This fire was a beauty to probably three or four feet wide and five to six feet high. Well this old guy, who my father did not like too well, grabbed my arm. And that dog leapt straight through those flames and bit this guy's ankle and set him right back. No one could believe it even the guy that got bitten stood stock still. Mind you he was ordered to by the dog.

Mum had to patch him up and be all apologetic. Come to think of it mum did most of the apologizing. And yet with family he was the most gentle of all the dogs I've known.

We also had an old galah who went most places on foot. Now, ever since that pesky dog came on the scene he'd been an annoyance to the old bird. We called him Jock and he never took much to flying, we suspect it was a flying accident that put him on the ground with a broken wing when we came upon him.

Anyway old Jock spent a lot of time under the car with dad who always seemed to be under there fixing something. Consequentially the poor old blighter was always dirty; he'd just get covered in oil and grease. But we couldn't keep him out from under there it seemed to be his favorite place. He was a happy bird though and he could talk probably a little too well. Especially the swear words, they came out as clear as a bell. And you can imagine what his vocabulary was like spending all that time with dad fixing cars.

One day there in Peebinger an old lady, a bit stuck up, came to visit mum. None of us liked her so the Skipper remained on the chain. Dad was under the car again and didn't take to kindly to mum telling him no swearing. Jock screeched at her and put his head on the side to peer up at her.

The visit went off without a hitch. Then as our visitor was leaving old Jock walks up with his funny waddle, his head on the side squinting up at mum's visitor and swears at her. Mum's face goes bright red and she tries to shoo old Jock away. But old Jock has been hangin around under cars with dad too long and he side steps mum and screeched more obscenities at mum's guest. So mum straightened up and tries to tee he it off like while she ushers the woman away from the bird . . .

This old biddy stops though, she looks down at Jock and she say's 'Ooh what a dirty looking old tramp of a bird' and she had her nose stuck up in the air to. Well then she turned around to walk or should I say, march off, mum staring dumfounded at her. Now Jock who has been hangin around Skipper too long races in head down at her heals. His beak is open ready for the kill. Right at the last minute mum aims a slipper a big men's' slipper, at him and he goes down fighting and swearing at this bloody slipper. Did some bloody damage to the slipper to I'd hate to think what he would have done to her skinny heals in her nice pink scuffs and fine stockings.

So anyway the dog and the bird had what you might call an uneasy truce mostly but that dog just had to stir him up. Seems like there was a never ending string of curses from Jock, hurled at Skipper on a screech. He'd run after the dog but he never caught him and poor old Jock just wanted to be left alone. Sometimes Skipper would creep up on him while he was napping and he'd bark in his ear or grab his tail feathers. Poor old Jock always seemed to be picking up his own tail feathers.

Dad called us kids into the van one day and told us we'd be moving on so get packed. Get packed! We threw our footy in the back of the land rover.

When all the load was packed into the back dad would throw a tarp and a mattress for us kids to ride on up on top of the load. Then old Jock would be stuck in a bird's cage and chucked up there as well. Then old Skipper would come up and sprawl out and go off to sleep till we stopped somewhere.

This one trip we were on Judith and I were up on top of the load and Skipper was sprawled out between us sound asleep. We didn't realize it but Jock was sitting in his cage, deathly still with baited breath waiting for skipper's tail to fall just a little bit closer to the bars. And of course inevitably it did and Jock was in for the kill and he held nothing back either. Boy I tell you those beaks can cane when these little rats want to use em.

It was bloody bedlam up there Skipper gave an unholy howl and eyes bulging in pain and fright, leapt away from the cage and clear over the side of the rover. He was still somersaulting as he went out of sight behind the van Dad jumped out and demands to know what all the commotion was about I mean we couldn't stop laughing and Jock was screeching and doing his victory strut up and down his perch.

Well dad looks back at Skipper who's sitting on the side of the track licking his tail. 'Well I'll be buggered' he says 'good on ya Jock.' Then he looks at Skipper whose still sitting lookin all dejected and says 'well a run might do you good' and he drove off and left him.

Well the old dog ran off his resentment to Jock and Jock'd had a little win. We picked up skipper who went back to sleep facing the other way and by the time we made camp that evening all was forgotten.

Except that Skipper had to sit through another telling of the story and more laughter around the campfire that night as dad even told some fellow campers of his disgrace. Lucky Jock was asleep and so did not get to witness his humiliation. Thank God for small mercies as my mum used to say God rest her.

The last time I saw Skipper he was laying in the dirt with a bullet in his head because blue heelers cannot get along with sheep, and I bear his killer no malice. We kept his collar for many years in remembrance of an old and loyal friend. And I must say that life was emptier without him and when jock died of some strange cough he'd picked up a few months later it was the end of an era.

Thank you for letting me get this off my chest, many eras have gone by since and some of them have been bloody good. Some not so good and now I have three Chihuahuas. I often wonder what Skip would have made of these strange little creatures. I think we know what Jock would have done. No doubt one day we'll tell a story or two about them with their tiny bodies and their huge hearts.

Cheers till the next camp fire and we'll tell some more yarns 'ay.

# Chapter 19

# THE DRUM THAT BEARS THE CROSS

I straightened up and wiped the sweat out of my eyes and away from my face. It was December and it was hot. I'd been trying to get this damned chiller started since early morning. I looked up at the noon day sky, my poor frying brain trying to figure out why the old girl just wouldn't fire up. I dropped the crank handle in the dirt and slumped against a forty four gallon drum. Everywhere you looked was bare red sand, not much green around now. Rabbits would be gone soon and so would we. We needed rain.

I looked back at the old diesel motor a sinking feeling in my chest. If I couldn't get this chiller started then all the rabbits would go off and no one gets paid for rotten rabbits. The stress!

I looked up towards the house, not much point going back up there I thought dismally. It was the day after Christmas and my dad had been on a bender now for three days and by my calculations he had enough grog left to stay on it another three.

126

My brother shot passed me on his bike he got for Christmas and blew me a raspberry and called me a name. A real charmer that one. I thought I'd take a few minutes to amuse myself making sure and certain my brother's life was just as miserable as my own. Too easy!

I went round the side of the old shearers quarters we'd pulled the van up next to so as we could use the water and waited for the boy to ride on passed. Hidden between the tank and the wall I settled in to wait. I didn't wait long, about fifteen minutes and for an old hand at hunting like myself, that's nothing.

He rode up and just as he was about to pass me I jumped down and roared at him. That was enough, his nerves did the rest and he twisted the handle bars and over went the bike into the red dirt with him on it. He was six and he was still a pain in the proverbial. I cast a practised eye over him to see if he had anything to go and show mum but he didn't. I left on the bike.

Now I won't pretend that it was my opinion that the dress I got for Christmas stacked up against the bike and the slug gun he got because it wasn't. I was sore. And to make matters worse it was a very pretty dress and I knew I would be expected to wear it to the Tibooburra New Year's Eve ball. I was strictly a jeans girl.

Ball! A two piece band in the old town hall played mostly out of key and everyone there thinking it was their own fault about the two left feet because they couldn't dance very good. A crowd of ringers fighting in the main street for those who wanted some excitement. They seemed to dance ok.

The pub was right next door and while drunks staggered between the pub and a quick grope on the dance floor all us females were lined up round the dance floor to sit and wait and see if anyone ever picked you, Anybody remember that? I never found it very hard to get em to walk on by even at thirteen. But mum and dad seemed to like it all right but mind you they could always go back to the pub and . . . Still who am I?

So off I went on his bike to let off some steam. About five minutes and I was bored, my brother still calling me names from the back of the old sheds. I rode back to him. I had a long sapling stick in my hand and I knew what my mother could do with one of those and he knew I knew. He looked nervous. 'Run!' I said.

His mouth dropped open and he started to turn. I was getting closer and I heard him mutter something as he took off.

'You still callin' me names hey Bruce?" I asked. I was getting closer and pretty soon I gave him a good whack across his butt and he squealed and tried to go faster. Anyhow I took pity on him and decided to let him go.

I set off for one more ride before returning to the chiller.

I hadn't gone all that far when I decided I'd better get back to it and turned around to come home. About half way back I met my little brother coming to meet me. He sang out some pretty salty profanities at me so I took off after him. He ran like a scolded cat all the way back to the chiller. A chiller is a mobile freezing unit to keep the rabbits

It was just on dark and I was pelting along. In my intent to catch him I didn't notice him duck as he ran in between two big drums and I didn't see the rope he'd tied in between em. Not til it was too late anyway. My turn to pick myself up out of the dirt. I decided it might be best if I let him have a little win and went back to the chiller. I didn't get it started that day but I did find out what was wrong with it. I decided I'd fill her up with diesel tomorrow and went to bed.

'Which drum' I asked dad next morning? I'd slept late and he'd got a head start on me and wasn't making much sense.

'The one with the cross on it. The so'n'so diesel is always in the drum that bears the cross.' He stood looking at me with bright eyes one of em half shut as was usual when he was inebriated.

I turned round and went outside to fill up the motor. It wasn't easy but I did get the tank filled up, stuck the lid back on and grabbed up the crank handle. I began to turn it, round and round we went.

Now this particular crank handle sometimes decided to stay put for a while when you got her started. And then hopefully she stayed put long enough for all present to get down and grab dirt because sooner or later that handle was coming off and when she did it came at high speed. A smack in the right place would knock you clean dead.

Once again I grabbed no dirt that day because she just wouldn't start up. I tried till I was beat. Back up to the house to see dad.

'Dad I think its petrol in that drum.' I says.

'Which bloody drum?'

'The one with the cross on it.' I said

'Well if you got it out of the drum with the cross on it then its bloody diesel. Would you like me to repeat that for you?'

'Yep' I said and went back to it. And I repeated this procedure until the next day and daddy dear got redder and redder.

'If you got it from the drum which bears the cross then it is bloody diesel!' was all he could say.

I sat for a while the next afternoon knowing I had to do something soon the rabbits would defrost any time now. I kicked an old fruit tin across the red dirt and had the most amazing idea. I grabbed it up. Then I filled it up with the so called diesel. I'll show him I says to myself and off I went to see him.

Dad, who was standing just inside the door, snorted as I came in. The kitchen was hot because mum had a fire going in the stove to cook dinner. I smiled sweetly at my father and said in a cold voice 'sniff this. I tell you its bloody petrol.'

The tin was snatched unceremoniously from my grip. 'Pig' I said and took a step back.

'I'll show you' he said 'once and for all; I'll show you its diesel'.

I stood stock still, not even breathing I don't think as I watched him walk the length of the old kitchen towards the old wood stove the tin of petrol clasped firmly in his hand. It dawned on me what he was going to do but I was having trouble believing. And he didn't stagger or bump into anything, as straight as a die he walked the length of that kitchen.

It was over in seconds. He lifted his hand and slung the contents of that can into the flames. For the briefest time he seemed to disappear. The, cast iron plates of the stove top seemed to leap into the air in a whoosh and a bang. With a crash they settled back onto the stove top. Dad seemed to have frozen as the lot went up right in front of him and didn't immediately turn around. The kitchen was quiet once more.

He turned round slowly head lowered looking at the can as if he was studying it. He lifted his eyes to mine his eye lashes and brows singed and his hair in front sticking up and curly where the flames had licked his face. His face was the colour of a ripe strawberry. And not only that, he was sober!

'Yep' he said, 'it's petrol alright.'

Well I didn't say a word for once in my life and as I left the kitchen I knew I would not forget this day in a hurry. And I also tried not to laugh because if I did I might never stop.

I found the drum of diesel by the by and got the old girl started and I beat the crank handle into the dirt. I saved all the rabbits and got not a jot of thanks. But anyhow that's life aint it, you do what you can and worry about what you can't.

# Chapter 20

# THE MALLEE SCRUB

We arrived at Peebinga in the spring of '61; my father was trapping rabbits for a man down there who shall of course remain nameless. Peebinga was a little place, just a shop and a school and house or two.

It was only a short distance from Pinnaroo. Although none of us liked the place we were used to the open terrain of the sand hills, we stayed there for almost a year, the longest we ever stayed in the one place. I was seven when we got there and my sister was ten.

Incidentally I went to my first carnival while we there, Oh the rides the Ferris wheel the bucking horse. Not to mention the fairy floss and pop dogs. I suppose you might have guessed I joined my sister in sick bay all the way home. And dad who'd made too many trips across to the pub. What a miserable sight we were all sitting in the back, mum not speaking to us. Mum drove home nice and warm in the cabin with Bruce who was just a baby. Such is life hay; you live and learn.

We had to go to school; we'd never been as we had always done correspondence. I shall never forget my first day, the kids ran round us in a circle singing 'who wants to play with the trappers kids the trappers kids the trappers kids' and so on, you get the point. They were all farmers' kids except for the teacher's kids but they were all related in some form or another. Everyone was everyone else's cousin you know.

We just looked at one another, we'd known unkindness before. The human spirit can be a bit cruel sometimes. I like to think it's what we do between all the kindnesses we do.

Well there they were givin' it to us bumpkins alright, gypsies they called us. But they hadn't reckoned with a smart mouth like my good self.

I turned to the teacher's kids and said well who in H . . . would want to play with the teachers kids?' I showed my teeth the best I could. They faltered and stepped back a pace or two.

That showed em. I'd stirred up a hornets nest this time. My sister, in time was included in some of their games but not I. Not until Judy stayed home from school sick.

I hated that school and yet I was fascinated by it as well. I had never seen such a place. It was just unfortunate, I think, that back in those days the teachers could belt you as much as they liked with whatever they liked, whenever they liked.

And if you went home and told you'd just get another because smacking was considered good parenting then.

One time he came into the class room and announced to all, that he'd be giving us a test every Friday from now on. Ok I thought. And he went on to say that whoever got ducks of the school (the highest marks) he would give six pennies to. Music to my ears, my family had always told me how bright I was I'd just work extra hard. So I had that sixpence spent before he sat his skinny, butt back in his chair. I, after all, was in grade three.

Inevitably Friday rocks around and we all sit the test. Easy! Inevitably I win the sixpence; the lousy trapper's kid got the sixpence. Me? All I could think about when he dropped the sixpence silently in to my hand, his moustache twitching like mad, was the look on mum's face when I gave it to her. My, she'd be pleased, and proud.

And I won the sixpence the next week and the next and so on. No problem. I went to the shop and got a half a loaf of bread for mum with the sixpences, back then the bread was not sliced. To get half a loaf the full loaf was pulled apart and there in the middle was all this fluffy, white fresh bread. And I was allowed to pull this fluffy bread off and eat it on the way home, the loaves I bought with my sixpence that is.

Once mum handed the sixpence back to me and told me to go spend it. Lollies! The teacher's wife ran the shop and she was not at all pleased for me. She had mauve coloured eyes and she never spoke to me.

But then I started getting the cane for the damdest things even when I was accompanied by others I alone took the fall. I was never bright enough to comprehend that the belt always followed the sixpence. Anyway.

In the end the teacher strode in one day and told us there would be no more sixpences. My disappointment was complete.

Anyway the favourite game in the playground in that school was football. Every lunch time the kids would get out and two captains would pick their teams. It happened that there were an odd number of kids in that school so I never got picked. My sister did but I did not.

I sat everyday on the side lines wishing I could play. I prayed they'd pick me, I lined up every day with the others hoping they'd pick me. They did not. Of course by this time I'd become somewhat of a laughing stock on account of the bike I rode to school on.

It was a small bike just like the BMX bikes of today but back then they hadn't been heard of. It was a small bike with thick tyres and my dad said it would be better in the sand. It was. And then one day I hurried back to school to see if I'd get picked and had not wiped the egg off my face apparently from my lunch.

Well the usual welcoming committee were out to watch and laugh at me rock up on my little bike and the egg on my face caused a riot. The kids were having a good old laugh at me and started singing egg face, egg face egg face. Well I levelled my most disgusted look at em and replied 'egg face yourself egg face egg face egg face.' As soon as I'd said it I knew today would not be the day I'd get picked either.

After about two months of this carry on I got my big break. Judy had stayed home sick from school and so that left an even number of kids in the school, you follow me? I knew I was in! And yep, I fronted up and got picked.

I couldn't believe my luck as I strutted out onto that oval with the others, most of whom towered over me. The captain of my team, incidentally the teachers' boy, sent me down to go goalie. Goalie! Off I went to do my damndest and to show em I could do a better job than that bloomin' Judy.

I could run faster than her to although she was a year or two older than me. I knew this because I always beat her when we ran from Roly Slattery's blue healer.

Sometimes on the way home from school a handful of us kids would swing by to tease Rolys' dog which was always tied up and asleep under the caravan at that time of the day. He was a deep sleeper and we could sneak right up on him.

The fun part was that he was on a very long chain and when we rattled a stick under the caravan he'd come out like a shot out of a gun teeth bared and growling worse'n any big wolf. We had to beat him to the end of the chain. He'd forget his chain and when he came to the end the damn thing'd yank him clean off his feet he ran so fast.

I remember one day me and some of the other kids decided we'd have a bit of fun with him. We rattled the stick, out he came and off we ran. And ran and ran.

'The bloody things off the chain for Christ sake' somebody yelled as frightened kids went in all direction. Blind terror kept us goin that day and leant wings to my feet . . .

Anyway down to the goal square I went with my little chest puffed out, wishing mum and dad were here to see this. And who knew, do a good job today and well . . . .

Somebody threw the ball up and we were off. My team had the ball I knew that but then it changed hands a few times. I tried to keep abreast with it and finally it got all the way down my end of the field. Suddenly the teacher's kid had it and he kicked it to me and shouted 'get the ball Mary'.

'Right' I agreed, didn't have to tell me twice. I got the damn ball; I got it in my hands my heart thumping like shit. This is gonna be easy I says to myself as I ambled up to the goal and kicked it through. A big shout went up and in my dilemma I thought I heard somebody questioning my mental prowess. Someone else made reference to the idiot rabbit trapper's kid. Couldn't be!

In those days and in that place the rule was that if you kicked a goal for the other team it stood as a goal. It counted as a goal. I couldn't believe nobody had told me about this, I had disgraced myself and blown probably the only chance I'd get to play footy with this lot. I had picked up the ball and instead of saving I kicked the bloody thing into the other team's goal. I had misunderstood 'defence'.

And at the end of the day we lost by a goal and my football career was over. I consoled myself in the knowledge that as soon as the numbers evened up again I would have been out anyway.

And for the record I have always loved the game and I watch it every weekend and yes I barrack for the Crows. Or Port Power, whoever's playing. It's a hard game now footy I think, and these guys are so tough. And I guess after my effort I can't really criticise can I? You win some, you lose some, see you all again someday in the great outdoors.

## The End

# Chapter 21

# THE CHILLER HILL

For those who don't know, the chiller hill was the last hill we crossed before we reached the chiller. And at the chiller were two families of kids to play with and Mr and Mrs Brown. Out there it was a bit of a rarity and somewhat of a luxury to have kids to play with. I reckon that's probably why I grew up a bit of a loner.

I was four and a half; almost five at this particular place and my sister was turning eight. Rightly or wrongly I was insanely jealous. How I longed to be eight. I mean these were exciting times, indeed they were It was after the war and society had already changed so much.

Rock and roll had taken the world by storm and no doubt was here to stay. Rolf Harris sang his heart out with catchy little tunes like 'Tie Me Kangaroo down Sport 'and even got away with a song about Jake the Peg, with his extra leg. While Bill Haley and the Comets Rocked Around the Clock, Elvis Presley with his sweet, velvety voice made us believe he didn't have a wooden heart and Lonny Donigen's old man was a dustman.

Whilst it was some peoples bag to do the stomp Chubby Checker had the rest of 'em trying to keep up with the twist. The radio was blaring out music that was uplifting and made you feel lucky to be alive. Great times indeed.

The radio also kept us amused and entertained with serials; soaps like Portia Faces Life and Doctor Paul. And who among us didn't tune in at least once to the very famous Blue Hills. I grew up believing they were a real family. And let's not forget the comedies, to name a few, Life with Dexter and Green Bottle and even Stepford and son. I wonder how many people knew that Step ford and Son was on radio here first.

We all tuned in to listen to different ideas on the talk back shows that sprang up around the country and the ever changing face of the news kept the country better informed than ever before in the history of the world.

The game shows kept us amused and thinking, when they came into being on the radio. I remember Pick a Box and Bob dyer had such a way with people and I think Jack Davies to from memory.

Late night scary shows were popular especially with kids, we were allowed to wait up on one night of the week for Creaking Door. And all the afternoon kids' shows had us inside with our ear to the radio, the focal point of the family. And even the ads, which we all whinge about now, were new and exciting. Colgate left us with a ring of confidence, Laxets kept us active and vegemite kept us happy not to mention how much we liked airplane jelly, for tea or any other time.

Girls' hem lines were going up and up and who knew where it would all end. Also girls and women were staying at work longer as opposed to getting married right away and some even went on to become career girls. The war had opened the door to new possibilities for women, my mother worked in munitions. We used to joke about how mum made the bullets and dad fired them. Dad was a world war two vet and a hero to boot.

During the war the fairer sex had taken on the work that the men were not here to do. They had also taken a liking to the freedom that working gave them and they liked the workplace, par say, better than the kitchen. The pay was better than ever and the women liked the notion of being independent. By the time the men got home to take back their jobs they were in for a fair bit of opposition.

Not only did this new woman want to keep his job but she wanted equal pay! She got the vote! These men, returned home from the war themselves in disrepair, found a very different kind of woman home to greet him. They were taking on careers in medicine and law and some of them even went into politics.Yep, the times they were a changing alright and I think that was Bob Dylan.

Boys were wearing their hair longer and taking a bit more of an interest in their appearance. Suddenly he had to compete for her affections. He had to compete not only with other chaps but with her new found independence.

Girls and boys together was anybody's guess. The rules were changing all over the place. I think the pill may have, in my opinion, had the single most profound effect on this area of life. It was liberating, girls were free to do what they wanted with whom they wanted and thanks to the pill they could kid themselves no one knew.

Suddenly babies were something people planned not dreaded. How much of a change do you reckon that would have made in people's lives all over the world? And people were actually starting to marry when they were ready and not because they had to.

And then, wonder of wonders, women started going to the courts for a divorce if she so desired. Madness and mayhem! And I take my hat off to that brand new, gutsy style of woman who braved the scandal and changed the world.

People sang about the war and everyone was eager to put it behind them. I guess singing about it helped to put it to bed. And being poor didn't hold the same terror for people after Hitler and his brand of terrorism. How terrifying was it for people when the Japanese flew in from the north for their say. After the depression hunger was on the decrease and windcheaters were invented to keep us from the cold.

Anyhow I'm sure you get the point as to how it was a bad time to be four and a half. Anyway back to the story, I do prattle on I think it still excites me.

This one time we came over the chiller hill and we all sang out at once that we were the first to see it. We went straight to the chiller on this day rather than going straight to the Whitefields. Dad got out and one of the men came over with somewhat of a worried grin on his face. We all got out of the car to go and visit and leave dad to unload the rabbits. Before we could do this however Gordon indicated the Browns' tent with his thumb and said 'they're havin' one of their rows again.'

Is everybody alright?' Dad asked as he jumped out of the rover.

'Yeah' says Gordon, 'they'll work it out.'

We all stopped and sort of braced ourselves against the very bad language that was coming from that tent. See, the Browns, Mary Brown and Mr Brown, often had these squabbles and mostly no one took any notice.

Today was a bad one, Dad stopped what he was doing. I mean Mary Brown would have been in her seventies and she was a very skinny woman about five feet one; and she wore natures map etched deep in her leathery skin. Mrs Brown would have been about the same but a couple of inches taller with fewer stories told on his face.

The centre pole of the tent was waving around wildly as the conflict got more physical, and as I watched in horror, it gave one final lurch and down she came. Down on top of the happy couple inside.

They were still at it, worse if anything, well louder anyway. Some of the onlookers laughed, I mean it looked so funny. As the slight form of Mary Brown groped about trying to get out the other, Mr Brown tried to get hold of her and stop her. She got away and out she came trying to get her mop of crazy hair out of her eyes.

And here's where Mr Brown made his big mistake, he stopped for a spell.

Mary Brown got the hair out of her eyes and ran straight to the fire where she had left a big heavy based frying pan. And I believe she meant to fry him. Everyone stood motionless mouths agape but silent while Mary Brown went about beating up Mr Brown. Every time he put his head up she hit it with the pan.

Just as she was finding her stride a huge whirly wind came through and I'll be damned if it didn't blow Mary Brown clear off her feet; she was so tiny. It was one of the funniest things I've ever seen. The whirly hit the pan as she lifted it up in the air for another shot at him. Mary Brown would not let go. She staggered backwards a few steps and then measured her length in the dirt. Well, women's Lib. had made its debut in the great Australian outback.

I know I take my hat off a lot but if I may indulge myself one more time; I would like to take my hat off to these truly unique, pioneer women who followed their man into the great outback of Australia. No one could ever say you were looking for an easy ride and I have only some idea of how strong you had to be.

I know that out there in that country in its entire splendour, danger and hardship, you had to have nerves of steel. And if you didn't well then it was your bad luck you just had to deal with it on your own. Long periods of time, in some cases months and months, all alone with only yourself to rely on.

Dust, heat and flies, pain and sadness, hard physical demands of staying alive and raising your children. By yourself! But you made it you had the tenacity to overcome all obstacles. Bravo ladies, great stuff!

In fact I would even go so far as to say that when man walked on the moon; when he first set foot on the moon, and looked down upon the earth, it was a woman who sent him there. Whoops! No really to all of you women out there who brought us into the world I say thank you and God bless you.

And to our fathers who had to be even stronger at times as they fought against hardship after punishing hard ship; thank you from the bottom of my heart the ride was truly great! Not always fun but great. May I just say that I wouldn't trade my upbringing for another's.

Maybe we'll all meet once more in that great outback beyond the stars and of course we'll tell some more yarns hay.

# Chapter 22

# IN GOD WE TRUSTED

We'd come to the end of the road, we were out of food and almost out of water and the four wheel drive, our only vehicle, had a broken axel. We were located up north of a place called Starvation Corner. Poeppel Corner to be exact. The place was the corner country where the south Australian and Queensland and N.T borders meet. And we were alone, something you should never do out in that country because people died out there. So we usually travelled in groups, but not today.

It was summer and most of the wild life had gone south and the vegetation was very sparse. Just those tough old mulgas a few spinifex bushes and what grass there was; was drying fast. It was truly a god forsaken country right now.

The red sand hills were almost bare and the slightest breeze raised a dust storm. A wind would whip up dust clouds you couldn't see through and had to wear rags over your face so you could breathe. Anytime you had to go out in the heat of the blistering sun you'd get fine red sand in your shoes and it burnt. It just got in everywhere that sand.

The thing about that country out there, it took just one good rain to transform it into the most beautiful bush lands in the world. Overnight it would spring to life again. Beautiful wild flowers daisies grasses and the wildlife just came teeming back. And God was returned to the land of the outback.

On this particular day, my sister and I sat in the meagre shade of a mulga tree. The hot north wind blew relentlessly drying and burning everything in its path. You couldn't escape it as it dried and seared the back of your throat as you tried to breath. The hot sand it blew into you face stung and left it feeling like it had been sandpapered.

We had been on water rations for a week now and were not allowed to play or move around too much else we'd need to drink more water. We had a pretty fair idea we were in real trouble this time. It seemed that even the flies had deserted us in our hour of great need. It was sheer hell.

Food had been rationed for weeks and ran out yesterday. Nothing we could do now but wait for the rabbit cart to come with supplies and a new axel. And pray and hope he'd be in time. He was already five weeks late and our future was lookin bleak.

My sister and I were too weak to play and every movement was a supreme effort. I sat in the shade for a while then with a great effort I found my way back to the caravan. This I did with my hands and ears as my sight had failed me a couple of days ago. I was six years old.

I remember mum and dad telling us stories till late into the night to take our minds off the hunger pains until we went to sleep. And they were pains, terrible nagging pains that hacked away at your mind. After a while your body tuned on itself as the vomiting and diarrhoea took hold. Even if you did eat something you brought it straight back up or it went straight through.

I whinged to my mum as I tried to climb up into my bunk but I missed my footing and lay on the floor where I fell. My mind was as clear as a bell. If only I knew a prayer. Must learn one I thought absently and smiled at the futility of these thoughts.

My sister stepped over me on her way back to her bed and as little as I was I knew we had lay down to die. I heard my father mumble that he loved us as he slid to the floor. I felt sorry for him because I knew how very much he did love us and it must be hurtin' him bad.

Mum was out to it and apart from the occasional moaning we had not heard from her since dawn. I felt sad because I missed her and tried to inch closer to where she lay. I can only guess that my parents went down so quickly because they gave the bulk of the food rations to us. God love em'.

My last meal had been kangaroo meat boiled in water; we had even run out of salt. The cramps were agony. And to this day I will not put 'roo meat to my lips. The water we had to drink was hot except sometimes at night it cooled to lukewarm. And now we were too sick to hunt for food. Wasn't much about anyway thanks to the drought.

Mum had lain down, too sick to get up a couple of days back and dad had tried to keep us all going. I'd woken up the night before to the sound of his pleading voice as he tried in vain to make mum hear him.

I hated this and I wished it would all go away. As young as I was I knew I would soon get my wish, one way or another.

Out in the afternoon heat a crow cawed its lonely desolate note to the sky. It had a particularly mournful sound on this day as if he knew of our demise and just wanted to be of comfort. The sound was anything but; for I thought maybe he just waited for a feed. They were scavengers, it was their way.

The afternoon sun had dipped low on the horizon when next I opened my eyes. Must be close to tea time I thought, my hunger was worse. It always got worse at night. All I could see was shadows and light and the light parts had gotten dimmer. The air was less intense and the north wind had dropped.

We had slept all afternoon and my mind was groggy, and when I heard it I thought it was just my mind playing tricks. Maybe it was just the wind in a bottle. Before any of us realized there was a truck outside the driver was at the door.

I shall never remember the smiling face of Alfy Baites, but I shall always remember his cheery voice as he sang out 'anybody home?'

Dad got to his feet, he was groggy to but he said 'Jesus am I glad to see you, ya bastard.'

Alfy put his hands out to steady my father as he almost fell down the step into his arms.

'Christ' says Alfy, 'how long you buggers been out a' food?'

'Bloody days' dad replied, 'we nearly bloody died.' As if he'd just remembered, 'Alfy help me' he cries and hobbled up the step with Alfys' help.

He knelt down by mum and says 'the carts here Maida, we're saved.' He shook me and my sister and repeated this simple statement. 'We're saved.'

Then he was gone and he came back with a tin of peas and a tin of pineapple and we began to eat. 'Slowly' he told us 'nice and easy.' I sat on the floor, tears rolled down my cheeks and his as he fed me from the tin.

I can't remember what we ate next but I do remember the cup of tea dad made us and I do recall making a speedy recovery. Though my sight didn't return for a few days, don't know what that was all about.

Soon the truck driver bid us goodbye and went on his way farther north to pick up rabbits from a chiller up there. After a couple of days, he got his strength back a bit so dad changed the axel on the rover and he had us packed and out of there in no time flat. Not bad huh?

'Where are we goin dad?' I asked. Yeah things were back to normal.

'We're goin down south to Lake Eyre. The Windfords are down there.'

Now I must tell you here that the reason why the cart was so late was that the buyer dad was working for had gone broke. He'd sent supplies as soon as he could but couldn't send a whole lot. So we didn't have much but we packed what we had and headed south to join the Windfords.

We were one happy family as we headed south to the safety of having other people nearby. One hugely happy family, thankful to be alive.

Until we ran out of petrol about two days south, three or four days short of Lake Eyre. We had been saved to die again another day. But where there's life there's hope and the food and water went on ration again immediately. We were all still pretty thin from last time. Dad sat on the side of the road or should I say track, and put his head in his hands. It broke my heart to see him like that, to think he was gunna have to go through this again.

We climbed into our beds that night with that old familiar hunger pain once more in our bellies. As I drifted off to sleep I heard mum crying softly and dad trying to sooth her, the fear running deep in his own voice. I knew again the bloody terror of dying and it hurts.

We were only too well aware that if the rains came we would never make it out alive. Not even a four wheel drive could get us out of there and, more to the point; no one could make it in. No aces left.

As the sun rose in the sky on the third day on the side of that track we had breakfast early. Breakfast consisted of bread sops, pieces of bread with thin milk made from powdered milk, and some treacle mixed in a bowl.

After breakfast we were instructed to sit about and not use excessive energy. I sprawled out under a tree, I was tired and I'd quite given up.

Anyway I was busy figuring out what sort of a life I would be missing out on. Would I have had children? Probably not I thought. I was an ugly child, maybe they'd look like me.

Once again I was otherwise engaged and miles away when the Windfords snuck up on me. I heard dad shout and I sat up to look. The Windfords had missed us and had come over two hundred miles to find us. Thank God for good friends. We didn't hang about that day and got going as soon as possible.

We had no more trouble on our way down to Lake Eyre but my father swore he would have his day with a certain bloody rabbit buyer. 'Left my family to die in the desert the bastard.' He was on the verge of tears as he glared into the fire, 'I'll catch up with him.'

'I'll be right behind you Art', I'll be right behind ya.' Vowed dads' best mate Gordon. 'The mongrel should be hanged.'

It was just great to get to Lake Eyre and to be part of a small community again. Nice to feel a bit safer, nice to have other kids to play with. Lake Eyre was really something to see and we all stayed there for must have been about four months. Just until the rabbits ran out and we were off to find more. Another patch of Australia, another patch of rabbits. Rabbits were big business back in those days we even exported rabbits for meat.

He caught up with that buyer who shall remain nameless, except to say that his first name was Milton, just outside of Silverton about a year later. Dad knocked him none too gently to the ground and told him what he thought of him. Milton begged him for forgiveness from where he knelt and my dad turned to walk away in disgust.

Then Milton asked dad if he'd come back and shoot for him again. Dad laughed but I couldn't help but notice he went back and helped this Milton to his feet. I held my breath I really did I'd seen that gleam in his eye before. He reaches out and steadies the man.

'Thanks Arthur' he says. I took two steps back.

'My pleasure mate' says dad and delivers one hell of an uppercut to the jaw. Hell I didn't even see it and I knew what was coming. Milton lands on his back two steps from my feet, blood and teeth running down the side of his face. He wasn't makin much sense now.

Dad looks up at me a twinkle in his eye and says 'well come on' and strode off. I followed him back to camp. We never spoke again of that incident I somehow knew to keep my gob shut.

Some things are too hard to exact a price for I guess. What price do you put on the lives of your family? Anyway we breathed a sigh of relief, Milton was still alive and we were off on another adventure.

But that's another story, so I'll see you then and for now, keep smiling.

# Chapter 23

## EMU, KING OF THE DESERT.

An emu lay dead in the hot desert sun the hot north winds making short work of the rotting process. Sadly another little form lay close by, it had been trying to draw comfort from its dead mother. My eyes filled with tears and so did Dads and mums. My sister sobbed out loud but we were all too sad to move. It's what happens out here in this country when the rains don't come. Wild life ends up as bleached bones on the red earth.

'Its nature' said Dad, 'I know it's sad but . . . .' He walked away and so did mum.

'Nature's cruel' I said in a shaky voice, 'I hate nature'.

I was seven years old and I didn't know what I was saying. My grief was causing that old familiar lump in my throat and it hurts. Maybe if we'd got here sooner I thought. The bodies were a few feet from making it to water. Tragic!

I couldn't tell whether the movement I'd just seen was the wind or my imagination or what but there it was again. I walked around to get a better look at the little one.

'Did you see that' I cried at my sister whose mouth had dropped open to. 'Dad' I bellowed 'come here quick!'

Dad and Mum came to see what all the fuss was about.

'Look' shouted my sister 'the little ones alive. Can we save it Dad? Please?'

'It's nature.' Dad replied gruffly, 'these things happen.'

How many times I've heard that in my life. 'It's nature. We can't interfere with nature' men will say. What do you call bulldozing thousands of miles of rain forest? Or damning rivers clearing scrub chopping down trees?

Not to be put off I bent down and gently lifted the baby into my arms. It squirmed once and then buried its head in the crook of my arm. 'Oh the poor little thing' I cried.

'What are we gunna do with a baby emu' dad asked? His voice had gone all gentle and I knew we had him on the ropes. I went in for the kill. 'I'll look after it.'

'That's what you always say' says mum. I didn't take my eyes off dad. He looked at mum; she softened to as I forced the little blokes head up.

'Oh well, I suppose we can only try' says dad 'but remember it may still die. Come on then we'd better get it a drink.

That emu who we named Lucky, lived with us for a time until finally he ran off with a woman emu he met out on the Nullarbor near Cook in Western Australia. He looked back once and he was gone and I cried myself to sleep for a week at least,

One of the fondest memories I have of him was during the summer of '59 I think from memory. At the time dad had an old friend a goanna who used to swing by a couple of times a week for some rabbit livers.

Well he didn't much like the emu I suppose because of the time when he came up behind Luck startled the large bird and nearly got himself stomped to death. Emus are normally a relaxed sort of bird till they get a fright.

This day one of dads' mates stopped by on his way home from town, he'd been drinking all the way by the looks of him. To cut a long story short he did some more drinking with dad and staggered off to get some sleep.

He crawled into the back seat of his car and went promptly to sleep. Sometime during the next morning about sunrise he felt something bang him on his forehead. He opened very groggy eyes just in time to get another one in 'his left eye. See Ike had the standard four-wheel drive with no doors, no roof and no windscreen.

He told us later that he saw an ugly face as it struck him again and again. We all ran out of the van in time to see Ike jump out of his car and run towards us gabbling about something we couldn't make out. Lucky was right on his tail.

Just when it looked as if Ike might make it a rogue goanna came out of nowhere and ran right up his back. Ike let out a yell as he went down with that goanna riding him fair into the ground.

'You should've gone down sooner' said dad between laughs. All bushies know that goannas'll run up you, they think they're climbing a tree its thought. If you drop they don't have anything to run up see.

'Get that camel away from me. For god sake get this snake off me. Help!'

I noticed dad frown as he walked over to shoo the troublesome pair away from his friend.

'What you talkin about camel? You weren't bein chased by a camel. That was a goanna and an emu just brought you down.' He said and started to laugh again. It was funny.

After we'd got Ike away from the emu turned demon who still for some strange reason wanted to kill him, mum got us all a cup of tea. Then Ike told us his amazing story.

He'd woken in the night and sat up to get a drink of water. As he sat there drinking it he was startled by a noise just above his head which was strange considering he had no roof. Ike looked up and straight into the eyes of a big old camel. As camels are wont to do it spat in Ikes' face and ran off.

'You wanna give the grog away' said dad as he laughed on. It was funny.

So anyway, when he woke up to his beating he was a bit muddled up and thought it was that pesky camel back for round two.

'Why did that bloody emu attack me then? I never did anything to him' Ike said with wide eyes.

'Well maybe he don't like the smell of camel spit' says dad. 'The goanna's just ornery and waitin for some breakfast. I still think you should mix more water with your grog next time mate.'

Everybody had a good laugh about it and I guess we'll never know what those two animals were up to. Anyway that's my story and I'm sticking to it.

See you next time then and we'll have another yarn hay.

# Chapter 24

## BILLY GOATS GRUFF

I am very hesitant to tell this story as it involves a poor old animal who hadn't done us any harm, and shows myself to have a ruthless streak a mile wide as they say. It is not a tale from the sand hills exactly but whenever we left the sand hills it was just until we could get back up there. You know, all roads lead straight back to the sand hills for us.

There'd been a bit of a drought up north and the rabbits were gone so we'd come down south so dad could get a job on the railways just till things came good up north. In those days the railways was like the dole, when you were unemployed and had no money you got a job on the railways to tide you over. And that is how we ended up coming down to civilization as mum used to call it.

We hit Mingary in the winter of '64; I won the junior girls championships in the North East Combined sports day for the first time I reckon. My dad was what they used to call a packer or fettler and my sister and I had to go to school on the bus for a while.

Mingary was a railway siding all there was there were six houses a shop and a railway siding complete with stock yards.

Mingary also had a damn down by the creek and my sister and I used to go down there catching yabbies. We'd catch so many we'd go around the town with a big bucket full trying to give em away and some of those old yabbies were over a foot long. I never got game enough to pick one up I always used a stick to get em in the net and straight into the bucket.

Anyhow, this town came complete with an old billy goat who they say had been left behind by a tribe and had never caused anyone any harm so he lived quietly on the edge of town, eating grass and drinking from the dam. That was until we got there.

It must have been early spring when we encountered the old Billy goat for the first time. We were on our way home from yabbying and so we dropped the bucket and the remains of our lunch for him to eat. We set off for home at a nice brisk pace.

We didn't hang about as we were a little frightened of him. He was a huge animal with great horns and a long beard. I don't think we'd ever encountered anything like him. So it was we dropped the lunch and ran.

We started seeing that old billy goat wherever we went and he was making us nervous.

I had woken up on this particular morning with an idea to go catch some yabbies and take lunch with us. I jumped out of bed and woke my sister and she got up and got ready. Mum made us some sandwiches and told us to catch some yabbies; she just fancied some she said. We took some raw meat and some string and the net for catching them.

We'd been outside for about five minutes when my old friend joined us. He reared up on his hind legs and shook his head and my tummy dropped down to meet my bowls. I was ten; I mean I had no experience with such a creature. I'd been chased and terrorized by bulls as anyone who's read my stories will know, but this thing! I couldn't get a handle on him; I had not a clue where he was coming from. I do now of course and I think the poor old fellow just wanted some company.

'He's making me nervous' I told my sister. She nodded and looked behind her. 'Let's try and make him stop following us' I said ever hopeful of a good outcome.

'How?' my sister says without batting an eye lid. I felt a bit resentful I mean do I have to do all the thinking? Do I have to come up with all the good Ideas?

Let's get him to follow us' I says, 'down to the stock yards. Once he's in there, one of us will double back and lock the gate.' Swish! Mind like a steel trap and that believe it or not is what we did.

Once we had him locked up we made sure he had plenty of water and went yabbying without even a backwards glance. One thing I forgot to mention also is that seeing as how I had such a limited knowledge of these animals I had no idea they were such excellent climbers! I do now.

The next day was Monday, back to school. We got up at six-forty and left the house at seven-thirty to go across the road to get the bus. Guess who was waiting for us behind our back fence or should I say hiding behind our back fence concealed until we were almost upon him.

He reared up on his hind legs, another of my bright ideas bearing fruit right in front of my eyes. Could be he wants to follow us to the bus I thought feebly in my brain. His front hooves hit the ground and he put his head down and charged. No mistaking his motives now.

'Which way?' I screamed at my sister. This was her ballgame now I wasn't about to leave anymore prints on this wreck. She didn't answer as she left me standing there and made her way to the bus and I've not seen her move like that before or since. Darned if I could catch her.

Well this went on for a while, this running away and it became sort of a game of hide and seek only the game was deadly bloody serious. Every time mum sent us to the shop he'd chase us in there and butt the shop door till we came back out.

The end came about one day when the billy goat chased mum inside. She wore quite an expression on her face as she sallied through the door. 'Whoa' she yelled as she slammed the door and the billy goat crashed into it. 'Look out' she shouted as she slammed the wooden door. The Billy crashed into it again and then again and all went quiet. Mum stared wide eyed at the door for a few minutes, and we stared wide eyed at her. Somehow I didn't want it to come out, you know, what we'd done and all.

Now I don't know where mum gets her ideas from, same place I get mine I guess. She walks to the laundry and comes back with the broom. She caught me giggling uncontrollably.

'Oh cut out your silly giggling Mary. What the hell brought this on?' she says as she walks to the back door. 'Didn't I tell you to shut up? And be quiet I want to listen.' Mum puts her ear to the door, eyes like saucers. I just pulled myself together, tromping down hard on the giggles and watched. I couldn't even risk a smile, hell I tried not to breathe.

Mum stood there listening for a while and another bang on the door made her jump and set me off again. I mean this was too good and funny as . . . The giggles faded as Mum lifted her eyes to mine and she somehow knew I was involved in all this. 'We'll talk later' Jeez mum was getting agitated but I still thought it was funny.

All of a sudden mum throws the back door open with one of her famous 'I don't have to put up with this' as she throws back the screen door. The Billy goat was back at the fence now and puts his head down to charge see. Mum threw the broom at him and the billy goat threw his head back and mums broom sailed off harmlessly, so harmlessly, into the dirt. So once more he comes charging at the door. His head banged on the door just as dad came round the corner.

'What's going on here?' he asks with only a slight interest. The billy goat took off! A smile was making its way across dads face.

Mum told him. Dad threw his head back and laughed. Mum asked him if he thought it was funny and dad said 'Well . . .' Mum asked him how she was supposed to get the damn washing off the line if she couldn't go outside.

'Alright, alright I'll take care of it in the morning' he says and looked hard at me as the grin vanished from my face. Aw how do they know? I thought as I got my homework out on the table.

Well that's another story it's been good therapy writing about this. Mum never had that little talk with me so I got away with that, whatever it was. You know. I've been plagued with guilt. Well you know how parents tell you that Patch or Polly has gone to live on a farm. Sooner or later its gunna hit you where he really went. I never had the inclination to lock anything up from that day on. I guess I have come to realize also that the old Billy goat could have caught us anytime he wanted to but he was content to just frighten us to death.

I don't know if that dam is still there or not I know they knocked the town down and there's nothing there now. I will get back someday and have a look as it was teaming with yabbies. I guess the old billy goat still haunts the place and may I say how sorry I am that we had that stupid idea to lock the poor old beggar up. I need to tell him that to. Thanks for letting me get this off my chest; guilt gets a bit heavy after a while.

Anyway that's that mate, Hope to be able to tell you another yarn soon hay. Cheers.

# In Closing

I would just like to say a heartfelt farewell to all who have read my story or some of it. I miss these tales already it has been both a joy and privilege though sometimes a trial. I have laughed and cried as I wrote; nostalgia can be fun but also painful. Obviously some of the material was hard to bring out and air, people don't always understand. Especially hard is the fact that I do not know how this book of stories based on my life will be received and after all, these stories are me.

I have stuck to the truth as I recall it. Of course if I have offended anyone or any race, denomination or group of people I am sorry and you need to let me know if I have been unfair to anyone. It was never my intention to hurt another's feelings or put them down in anyway.

For the most part though this book has been such a fun thing to do, it's been a lot of laughs and brought good memories back to. But I must say that before I started writing these stories I never realized what a loser I am. As I sat back and read some of it I thought 'what was I thinking?' I mean what sort of a loser throws a dead dog over some body's fence or pinches grapes for the hell of it? We weren't that hungry. And what was I thinking giving my little brother a cigar? I could say that the only reason I did it was to put him off smoking but we all know that's not true.

I often wonder if my parents had known about some of this stuff, how worried they would have been about their little girl. Their little Mary girl as they used to call me.

Don't worry there's lots more where this came from. And I haven't got a whole lot brighter so there probably will be a second book. Maybe they won't allow me to print it! Don't worry I'll get it to you somehow.

Of course there are some very valuable lessons in there to. Not necessarily how to be a better thief, fighter or practical joker. No, and yet I wouldn't go quite as far as to say I learned anything about being a better sister or daughter or citizen. But I don't think I ever really looked for lessons as such I was always quite happy to just mosey along life's highways, ambling from one disaster to another. And I took my time about it.

I have met some truly great people along the way in all walks of life. There are people of all different sizes, colour and race and they are here among us. I wonder what they have to teach me.

I must say here to that I am not a very well educated person, not by today's standards anyway. I always had trouble at school; I'd just sit and look out the window, dreaming up more mischief.

And I have met all manner of people in my travels from miners, cowboys, criminals, artists, shearers, musicians, prospectors, prosecutors, teachers, doctors, dancers, electricians, farmers and truck drivers like my good self.

I have shared my table with many races and denominations All have eaten at my table along life's' way, or drank there. I have had the privilege of sharing their time and learning from them.

And do you know what I have discovered when you scratch the surface of such people? We are all the same. Same strengths and frailties, same fears and phobias. Different beliefs propelling us along the same paths.

Some of us have it bloody tough though and there are those poor souls among us who give up. And once more I take my hat off to all those people who have gone through so much more than their fair share of pain and hardships but they have picked themselves up time after time and dusted themselves off and got back into it. Back into life. And they have beaten their anger, overcome their fears, swallowed their pride and soldiered on to be decent caring honest people. Great stuff!

As for yours truly here, fifty five years on planet earth and I can't wait to get stuck into the next fifty odd. That is a truly scary thought; I'm only half way through and only getting worse! But life just gets better and better doesn't it? And it's true that you never know what's around the next corner, and that my friend could be a good thing or a bad thing. There are no guarantees, plenty of surprises, but no guarantees.

Well I am going to start on another book; I have to write so I guess you'll be hearing from me again. If you are reading this then we are mates so thanks again for all your help and for letting me get some things off my chest, I am grateful.

I'd like to say goodbye to you now and until we meet again somewhere in the great outdoors in this beautiful planet of ours, please look after yourselves and each other. So farewell and fair well from your humble servant. I am Rosanna Mary Seaton-Hoppo now of Pt. Pirie in SA. Great little place! Come and see us hay.

The End

www.ingramcontent.com/pod-product-compliance
Lightning Source LLC
Chambersburg PA
CBHW020413290526
45785CB00002B/540